This publication is designed to provide accurate authoritative information in regard to the subject matter covered and contains the opinion and ideas of its author. The author and publisher are not engaged in rendering medical, therapeutic or any other services in this publication to the individual reader. If professional advice or other expert advice is required, the services of a competent professional should be sought. Neither the author nor the publisher shall be liable or responsible for any loss or damage allegedly arising from any information or suggestion in this book.

ISBN: 978-0-9732167-5-2

Printed in Canada

This book is dedicated to the memory of David Martin, the founder of the Martin Clinic which is 100 years old this year. His legacy continues to the 4th generation of health care practitioners who have with the best of their abilities tried to follow in his footsteps.

Also to the thousands of patients who have made the Martin Clinic what it is today.

To God be the Glory

DAVID MARTIN

1873-1952

SERIAL KILLERS THE TWO HORMONES THAT WANT YOU DEAD!!

FORWARD BY CURTIS BELCHER

As co-host of “The Doctor Is In”, a locally syndicated weekly radio show that has received thousands of calls over the last five years, it has been an amazing journey to watch Dr. Martin deal with health and wellness issues with people from all walks of life. I have never met anyone with such a passion and depth of knowledge for proactive healthcare. Spend just a few moments with Dr. Martin, and you will be infected with his joy and passion for healthy living. His latest book “Serial Killers - The Two Hormones That Want You Dead!” exposes two hormones that have been wreaking havoc with our health. Unlike so many other authors, Dr. Martin does not simply bring to our attention the dangers that these “Serial Killers” present…rather, he arms us with the knowledge of how to arrest them!

There are few things more rewarding than seeing people’s lives change as a result of learning how easy it is to take better care of themselves when given straight forward no-nonsense answers about their health. Nobody does this better than Dr. Martin.

Northern Ontario is known around the world for its natural resources and precious mineral deposits, but one of our greatest gems is Dr. Tony Martin.

Curtis Belcher

General Manager of KFM Radio

Co-Host of “The Doctor Is In”

NOTE TO READERS

Why are we writing this book? We at Martin Clinic are concerned about your future.

Health Care costs in the USA alone are 2.1 trillion dollars a year. In Ontario where our clinic is situated, our provincial government spends 70% of its budget on health care. Ninety-nine million Americans suffer from some sort of chronic illness. However, 99% of government budget on health care is spent on fighting existing conditions and a mere 1% is on prevention.

According to the Institute of Medicine one out of five kids entering kindergarten are obese. There are 220 million diabetics worldwide. In the USA alone 26 million people are diabetic and even scarier is that another 78 million are prediabetic. Diabetes kills 3.4 million people a year.

A recent article in the Lancet said "Until 1990 Type 2 adult onset diabetes was rarely seen in young people, but no more." The total cost to treat diabetes alone in the USA has risen to 174 billion.

Obesity and Type 2 diabetes have joined forces ravaging the health of millions of people.

The average medical doctor (no disrespect intended) knows little about prevention. It is the first time in recorded history that the average person in North America knows more about prevention and nutrition than their physicians. Doctors are so busy today that their practice is reduced mostly to writing prescriptions and just treating symptoms. Houston, we've got a problem!!

So folks, we are in a quandary. North Americans need a huge paradigm shift. We first need to understand that we are standing on the edge of a cliff, health care wise. If we don't turn this ship around – disaster is looming!!

We don't care what your political views are. However, if you think that Obamacare or Universal Health Care (Canadian) is the answer to this crisis, you are mistaken.

Friends, this book is perhaps the most important book you will ever read. We will tell you what the problem is and why we are so sick today, but more importantly, what you as an individual should do about it!

The Martin Clinic

Dr. A.W. Martin

Dr. A.P. Martin

Rose-Marie Martin, R.N.

INTRODUCTION

I was watching an episode of Criminal Minds a few months ago. About half way through the program the FBI figured that they were dealing with 2 serial killers instead of just one. These two killers were copying each other and confusing the police. That got me instantly thinking of how two hormones-insulin and cortisol act the same way. INSULIN AND CORTISOL are the new serial killers on the block and they are wreaking havoc on people's health.

SERIAL KILLERS

Unfortunately it seems every couple of weeks we hear about serial killers-madmen who for no apparent reason just show up somewhere and start killing innocent people. From Muslim terrorists to individual nuts, it never seems to end.

THE TWO CULPRITS ARE INSULIN AND CORTISOL!

INSULIN

We have two hormones in our body that are very important but now have become serial killers. Insulin is a hormone secreted by the pancreas to convert a carbohydrate (bread, pasta, rice, pizza, pastries, fruits and veggies) into a simple sugar for energy. Unfortunately, since our diets are top heavy with carbohydrates we are secreting far more insulin than we need.

CORTISOL

Cortisol is another hormone- our stress hormone-that is secreted by our adrenal glands. Adrenal glands are the chestnut-shaped stress glands on top of our kidneys.

Whenever you are stressed, the body secrets adrenaline, cortisol and other hormones as part of our fight and flight mechanism. For example, if I scare you or sneak up on you-you are either going to have enough energy and strength to punch me or run away. Please run I don't want to be punched. That is the fight and flight mechanism. Unfortunately today, stress and moreover the secretion of cortisol in response to stress is affecting our population and destroying our health.

SO THIS BOOK IS ABOUT SERIAL KILLERS-HORMONES THAT ARE OBVIOUSLY IMPORTANT SINCE WE CANNOT LIVE WITHOUT THEM, BUT BECAUSE OF OVERUSE HAVE TURNED DEADLY.

THE PROBLEM-
THE OVERSECRETION OF THE 2 HORMONES
INSULIN & CORTISOL

PART 1

CHAPTER 1

CORTISOL

SERIAL KILLER #1

CORTISOL

SERIAL KILLER #1

"Adrenal glands are the body's very own Rodney Dangerfield. They get no respect."

Leigh Erin Connealy, MD.

Adrenal glands are two little organs on top of your kidneys that weigh less than one ounce. However, they secrete over 150 different hormones and are the body's first responders in times of stress. Adrenals make it possible to react to danger whether it is physical, emotional or even imaginary.

Adrenals are designed to have part time jobs. The demands of our current lifestyle have made stress an ongoing accepted part of daily life. The result - a non-stop stream of hormones flooding the body and eventually leading to fatigue and burn out.

The adrenal glands are key in several different body functions including:

1) Blood sugar and carbohydrate metabolism

2) Health of the cardiovascular system

3) Central Nervous System

4) Immune System

5) Hormonal Production

Here are the symptoms of adrenal fatigue and increase in cortisol secretion:

1) You are running on fumes and tired all of the time

2) Brain fog

3) Insomnia

4) Weight gain-especially around the belly

5) Anxiety or depression

6) Hair loss

7) Acne

8) Dizziness when standing

9) Nausea, vomiting, diarrhea

10) Loss of appetite

11) Craving salt or sugar-or both

12) Extra effort to perform daily tasks

13) Poor immunity

14) Reliance on stimulants like coffee to get going

15) Intolerance to cold

16) Feeling overwhelmed or crying

17) Feeling tired in the morning even though you have had plenty of sleep

If you have 3 or more of these symptoms your adrenals are secreting too much cortisol!!

CASE HISTORY

Ruth is a 40 year old patient that came to see me because she was exhausted all of the time. I would characterize her as a type A personality, meaning that if you want anything done-give it to Ruth. She has 4 children and a good marriage. Ruth told me that she used to have an enormous amount of energy. She kept herself in good shape by walking daily and watching what she ate.

Ruth mentioned that 3 years ago she was involved in a minor motor vehicle accident and since then she has always had recurring neck and back pain. She was also caring for a sick mother in the last few years who has just passed away recently. She was frustrated because she was gaining weight that she would have, in the past been able to easily lose-but no more!

Ruth had gone to several doctors to try to find an answer for why she was always tired. The same answer was always given-"all your tests are normal so you must be depressed." Her other symptoms included brain fog, sugar cravings and a decreased ability to handle stress.

Finally she heard about our clinic from a friend and decided to come for testing. Clinical results revealed Ruth had adrenal gland exhaustion with high secretion of cortisol and insulin. Ruth was given our Serial Killer eating program and within 6 weeks she is back to feeling her old self again.

"Avoid the standard blood test for adrenals (called the ACTH challenge). You can have lost 70% of your adrenal function and that test will read in the normal range."
Dr. Northrup MD.

CORTISOL AND BELLY FAT

Research has pinpointed the stress hormone cortisol as the key behind belly fat. Pamela Peeke MD. Author of "Body for Life For Women" says that "fat cells in the belly are especially high in receptors for both cortisol and insulin. Repeated stress insults add to fat storage in this region."

DOUBLE WHAMMY

Belly fat produces a stream of cytokines; inflammatory proteins that raise cortisol levels that disrupt blood sugar control, setting the stage for even more belly fat. Women who lower their cortisol levels by just 20% lose 9 times more fat and 30% more belly fat according to a study done at the University of Utah.

CORTISOL AND SLEEP

Cortisol skyrockets in people who do not sleep enough. Studies have shown that getting just 4-5 hours of sleep a night will boost one's CRP (C- Reactive Protein) levels by 75% according to Harvard University. An increase in CRP always means an increase in the secretion of cortisol.

ADRENAL GLAND EXHAUSTION

I think I was the first doctor to suggest that the new disorder (given names at the time like "Yuppie Flu", "ME" (Myalgic Encephalomyelitis"), "Adult Mono" etc. was indeed adrenal gland exhaustion. I am a pretty simple man and to me since we had never in medical literature seen this disorder before the early 1980's I came to some common sense conclusions;

> "There is a fatigue epidemic in our society" says Marcelle Pick author of "Are You Tired and Wired." "Eight out of ten women suffer from fatigue but since many doctors don't believe this energy draining condition exists millions remain endangered."

1) Chronic Fatigue Syndrome and Fibromyalgia was almost exclusively occurring in women.

2) The world as we know it has changed dramatically for women in the last several years.

3) Women in general are now under an enormous amount of stress as compared to women in my mother's generation.

4) Women today are stressed from all sides.

a) CHANGE # 1-WOMEN IN THE WORKFORCE

Today, women have to compete with men in the workplace. A WOMEN'S DAY NEVER SEEMS TO END. Women, by nature worry more and are much more detail oriented than their male counterparts. Remember, men come from another planet!! Women worry more about finances, relationships, children, their homes, their looks, clothes etc. This puts an enormous strain on their adrenal glands.

Remember, adrenal glands are stress glands on the top of the kidneys. These glands are made for stress, but they are not meant to be used 24/7. The stress glands should be used periodically.

Today the modern day woman is secreting cortisol like there is no tomorrow. Those poor little chestnut shaped glands are exhausted and the consequence is that most women are running on fumes-they are exhausted. In our previous book, "Energy robbers and the Fatigue Cure", we state that the #1 reason people visit their doctors is because of exhaustion.

b) CHANGE #2-WOMEN AND THEIR ENVIRONMENT

Is it not true that our environment has changed? We are surrounded by chemicals, plastics, fumes etc. Since World War 2 there has been 85,000 new chemicals created and the vast amount of them are found in our homes. From air fresheners, (I hate those things), artificial cleaners, anti-bacterial soaps, (I hate these things) carpets, pesticides, herbicides might have made our life easier, BUT, wow! Are we ever being bombarded and paying with our health?!! No wonder we are so sick and tired. I test patients every day for toxins and heavy metals and I can tell you that very few people escape from the effects of our modern environment.

WOMEN AND CHILDREN ARE CANARIES IN THE COAL MINE

Coming from a mining town (Timmins Ontario, Canada) and now living in another mining town-Sudbury Ontario, I can identify with the canary in the coal mine. The modern day women and children are especially vulnerable to changes in their environment. It seems that women's and children's bodies are a trap for aluminum, cadmium, lead and mercury that are often by-products of our modern way of life, from mercury fillings in teeth, fish, vaccines and sodas (high fructose corn syrup) to lead in jewellery, water and make-up.

CHINESE CONSPIRACY

I am usually not a conspiracy guy-no I do not believe that 9/11 was an inside job! However, I often wonder if the Chinese are not trying to take over North America:

1) They are lending money to the United States government. It seems to me that when you owe money to someone-they call the shots, ie: The bank, the Mafia.

2) They put lead in everything! Is it possible that the Chinese are slowly poisoning us with their toys and make-up? It seems to me that everything that comes out of China has lead in it! Lead is a highly toxic heavy metal that can lead to severe disorders such as Alzheimer's, depression, Parkinson's and cancers, just to name a few. Some Chinese food also has MSG in it that is a cancer causing food additive.

> Chronic exposure to increased cortisol due to stress is the primary cause of brain degeneration.

c) CHANGE #3-WOMEN'S FOOD

If you think that our stress levels and environment have changed-these are nothing in comparison to changes in our diet.

Most of our parents and grandparents were what we called meat and potato people. Today our nutrition is a far cry from what it was in those days. The average North American in the 21st century consumes 53 teaspoons of sugar a day. This is equivalent to consuming a 5 pound bag of sugar every 10 days! Amazing, isn't it? Sugar, by far is the #1 killer in our society today because it stimulates the over production of insulin and cortisol. From obesity to diabetes to ADD and ADHD, autism, metabolic syndrome, to high blood pressure, high cholesterol and asthma; all affect our health due to our changed nutritional habits. We are a "Carb Crazed" society and the vast majority of us eat very little protein and fat that are essential to our good health. Again, women and children head up the list of casualties when it comes to our modern diet.

SO YOU SEE FOLKS WHY OUR ADRENAL GLANDS ARE SO EXHAUSTED TODAY!

CHAPTER 2

INSULIN SERIAL KILLER #2

CHAPTER 2

INSULIN

SERIAL KILLER #2

Canadians and Americans have been sipping and slurping their way to a huge health problem. Obesity statistics tells us that as much as two out of three American adults are overweight and us Canadians are not far behind. This statistic represents a 30% rise just since the 1990's.

INSULIN-WHAT IT IS AND WHAT IT DOES

Insulin is a hormone that is secreted by your pancreas. Every time you eat a carbohydrate (bread, pasta rice, fruits, veggies, cookies and any other pastries, sugar or sweets) your brain sends a signal to the pancreas to release insulin. Insulin breaks the carbohydrates into a simple sugar that can be used by your body as energy.

The problem today is that we consume so many carbs, especially simple carbs (like sodas, pastries, doughnuts, cookies, muffins, bagels, white bread, white pasta and rice) that our pancreas works triple overtime to secrete insulin to break down these carbohydrates. Bottom line is if your insulin is high your chances of dying prematurely are greatly increased.

Most physicians do not routinely test for insulin levels. They just check for sugar in the blood.

THAT IS WHY INSULIN IS A SERIAL KILLER!

ELEVATED INSULIN LEVELS;

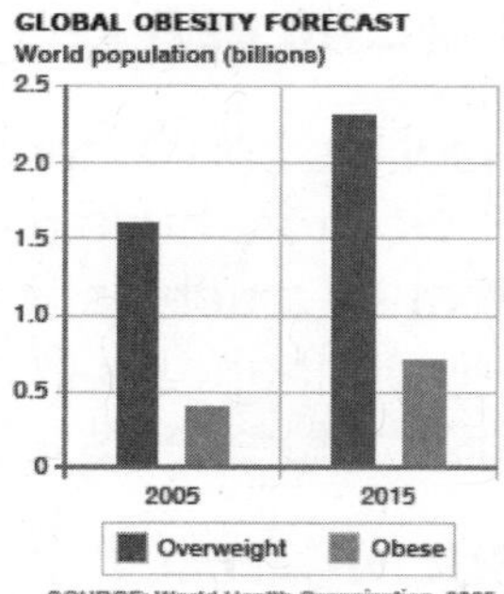

1) Interferes with the body's ability to break down fat.

2) Accelerates aging and increases the risk of Alzheimer's and dementia.

3) Increased blood pressure.

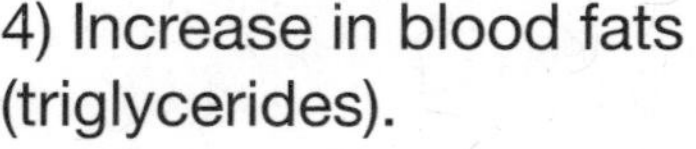

4) Increase in blood fats (triglycerides).

5) Increases risk of pre-diabetes and diabetes.

6) Increases obesity.

7) Increases risk of cancer.

8) Increases inflammation.

9) Increases risk of stroke and heart attack.

10) Increases risk of impotence.

11) Increases risk of metabolic syndrome.

METABOLIC SYNDROME

Elevated insulin is part of the Metabolic Syndrome coined by Jack Challem. When insulin is elevated there is a change that takes place at the cellular level which includes the cells ability to receive and process information.

Studies done by U.S. Department of Health Human Services estimate that 33% of American women now suffer from Metabolic Syndrome. This is a condition that essentially shifts the body into a fat storage mode and makes it next to impossible to lose weight.

At the heart of Metabolic Syndrome is insulin, a hormone that determines whether glucose is burned as fuel or stored as fat. Insulin is so key that many doctors have labelled the Metabolic Syndrome as IRS- not the Internal Revenue Agency but Insulin Resistance Syndrome.

CELLS GO DEAF

Years of high carb eating including S S & P-Sugar, Sweets and Pastries, breads, pasta, cereals and rice can result in the cell walls becoming deaf to the orders from insulin to open up, which causes glucose to build up in the bloodstream where it can end up damaging blood vessels and organs.

> The more one eats carbs, the more cells resist insulin, the more the body stores fat!

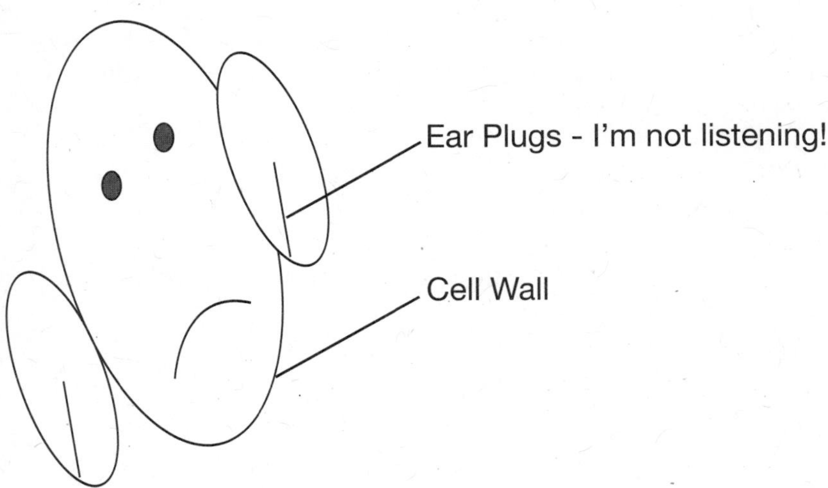

As a result the pancreas not knowing when to stop, secretes more and more insulin. The cells refuse to respond and open up, thus glucose is now stored as fat.

JIGGLY FAT AND INSULIN

A high level of insulin in the blood stream stimulates the formation of the "jiggly" subcutaneous fat that is located under the skin around the belly as well as the deeper visceral fat in and around the liver.

Belly fat is comprised almost exclusively of visceral fat. This type of fat can build rapidly since it fuels its own growth by disrupting blood sugar control and raising levels of fat storage cortisol. See how the two Serial Killers work together?

> Insulin is widely regarded as the fat storage hormone.

INSULIN AND SLEEP

Do you know that if you are not getting enough sleep your cells become more resistant to insulin? A recent study showed:

1) If you get only five hours of sleep nightly your risk of obesity increases 50%.

2) If you get only 4 hours of sleep your risk of obesity increases 73%.

The CDC says that 35% of Americans are getting less than 7 hours of sleep a night.

SLEEP

According to USA Today issue, March 23/11 if you are sleep deprived, on average you will eat more than 300 extra calories daily than if you are well rested.

If you get 6-8 hours of sleep you double your chance of hitting your optimum weight according to the Telegraph of March 29/11.

82% of American women are battling an excess of insulin that sends their bodies into fat storage mode.

The Martin Clinic believes that proper sleep is as important as good nutrition and exercise for weight loss.

By not getting enough sleep we put ourselves at risk for high insulin, high cortisol, accelerated aging, high blood pressure, depression and an increased risk of cancer.

Sleep deprivation negatively affects your leptin (your feeling full hormone).

How do you decrease insulin? Simply by: 1) Cutting back on carbs-especially Sugar, Sweets and Pastries 2) Getting more sleep

Remember, insulin is like a key that opens the cell wall to allow a carb to be converted to a sugar and stored in the cell for energy. However, if you do not use that energy right away the sugar is converted to fat.

So **INSULIN** is the key that opens the cell but also the key that locks the fat inside a cell. That is why it is so difficult to lose fat. On most diets you will burn water and muscle but you will find fat very stubborn. Why? Blame insulin. HELP! The door to my cells is locked and my fat can't get out!!

As fat cells grow they secrete inflammatory compounds such as Interlukin 6 and C - Reactive Protein. These bad guys damage insulin receptors on cell walls forcing insulin to remain in the blood stream.

Did you know that you should ask your doctor to do a C-Reactive Protein test? Why? If this test is positive it means that you are heading for big time trouble with either cancer or cardiovascular disease.

INSULIN RESISTANCE

With the high concentration of these insulin producing carbs our cells which need insulin to convert carbs to simple sugars start to develop a resistance. More simple carbs (bread, pizza) = more insulin = more fat. Insulin levels increase until your body's ability to make it wears out. High insulin levels are more deadly than high blood sugar levels because of the increased levels of cortisol and inflammation.

Did you know that insulin level improves if you have higher levels of Vitamin C? The Martin Clinic recommends 1,000-3000mg daily, especially if you are not eating enough fruits and veggies.

THIS IS WHAT I MEAN

A TYPICAL HEALTHY CELL

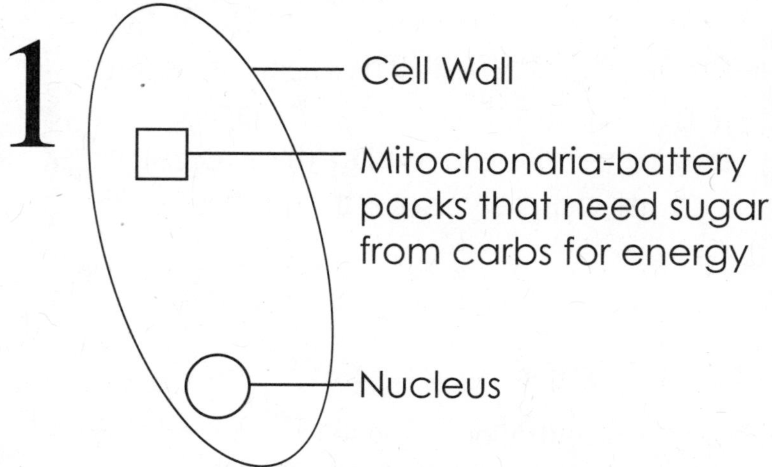

An increase in insulin also increases free radical damage-this leads to accelerated aging and an increased risk of cancer.

DIABETIC CELL

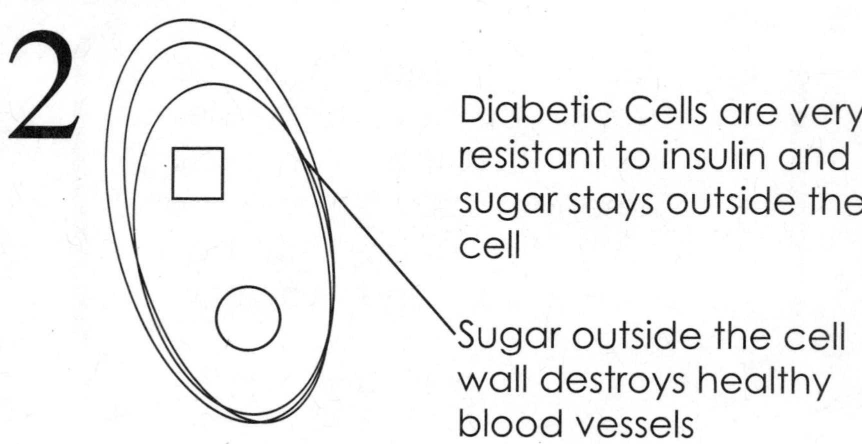

INSULIN

3

Insulin key that opens cell wall

TOO MANY CARBOHYDRATES

4

Cell Wall becomes resistant to insulin. The insulin key now has trouble opening the door.

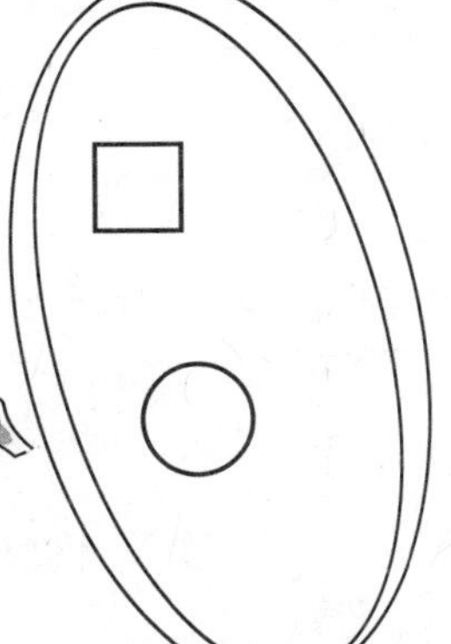

SIGNS OF INSULIN RESISTANCE

You know when your cells have become insulin resistant when:

1) You have love handles

2) You develop fuzzy or foggy thinking

3) You develop a pot belly

4) You have low energy

5) You have heartburn or acid reflux

6) You have a reduced low libido

7) You are tired after eating

8) You experience mood swings

> There is research showing that increased insulin levels will increase one's risk of breast, prostate and colon cancers.

Did you know that even a slight increase in circulating insulin levels makes one much more susceptible to heart attacks and cancer?

NOW YOU SEE WHY WE CALL INSULIN A SERIAL KILLER!

THE EFFECT ON THE BODY OF HIGH INSULIN PRODUCTION INCLUDES:

1) POOR CONCENTRATION

A classic sign of insulin resistance is fuzzy thinking. The chemical Orexin (found naturally in the brain) is linked with elevated insulin. Orexin seems to promote wakefulness and can cause sleeping problems when produced more than the body can utilize.

2) MOOD SWINGS

Range from grumpy and impatient to irritable and angry.

3) KIDNEY PROBLEMS

A continuous increase in blood insulin is toxic to kidney organs since one of their jobs is to filter out toxins.

4) EYE DISEASE

High levels of insulin make blood platelets sticky thus increasing the risk of blood clots. This is especially serious in the tiny blood vessels of the eyes, where it can lead to blindness, cataracts, glaucoma and macular degeneration.

5) NERVE DAMAGE

A) Neuropathy (a functional disturbance or pathological change in the peripheral nervous system.) The main function of the Peripheral Nervous System is to connect the Central Nervous System to your limbs and organs.

B) Bell's Palsy and Carpal Tunnel Syndrome are often related to high insulin levels.

6) SLEEP APNEA

There are three types of apnea:

a) Obstructive is the most common.

Obstructive sleep apnea (OSA) is caused by a blockage of the airway, usually when the soft tissue in the rear of the throat collapses and closes during sleep.

b) Central.

In central sleep apnea, the airway is not blocked but the brain fails to signal the muscles to breathe.

c) Mixed apnea, as the name implies, is a combination of the two.

Despite the difference in the root cause of each type, in all three, people with untreated sleep apnea stop breathing repeatedly during their sleep, sometimes hundreds of times during the night and often for a minute or longer.

With each apnea event, the brain briefly arouses the person with sleep apnea in order for them to resume breathing, but consequently sleep is extremely fragmented and of poor quality. Severe snoring is really sleep apnea.

7) ERECTILE DYSFUNCTION (ED)

Diabetes and pre-diabetes can be one of the causes of ED because of fluctuations in insulin levels.

8) BLOOD SUGAR FLUCTUATIONS

Blood sugar is needed for fuel. Our bodies make glucose by breaking down other types of sugar such as, table sugar, carbs (pasta and bread) and protein, (meat and fish). We were made to eat sugar and starches with fiber, the indigestible part of the plant. Fiber is found in veggies, fruits and grains and it slows down the digestion of starches and sugar leading to a gradual increase in blood sugar. Slow rise in blood sugar with moderate secretion of insulin is normal and healthy.

Pure sugars such as high fructose corn syrup, table sugar and white flour are digested quickly leading to a rapid increase in blood sugar levels. The starches in bread, pasta, pizza and muffins – S S and P (sugar, sweets and pastries) are digested quickly leading to a rapid increase in blood sugar. As your blood sugar shoots up, the body responds with insulin creating a yoyo effect thus making you hungrier.

A McDonalds Big Mac is 560 calories, 47 grams of sugar and carbs. A large fry is 570 calories, 70 grams of carbs. A Chocolate Triple Shake is 580 calories, 102 grams of sugar and carbs. This is a total of 219 grams of carbs in one meal!!!

CHAPTER 3

ESTROGEN

THE UNHOLY TRINITY

CHAPTER 3

ESTROGEN

THE UNHOLY TRINITY

Although estrogen should not be considered a Serial Killer per se it is still a major partner in crime. Estrogen in normal levels does the following for women:

1) Makes her feel more sensual.

2) Gives a glow to the skin.

3) Gives moisture to the eyes.

4) Lubricates the vagina

5) Gives fullness to the breasts.

6) Influences both the bones and the brain.

7) Brings clarity to the mind.

> Estrogen is to women what testosterone is to men.

Estrogen deficiency will cause:

1) Mental fogginess, depression

2) Mood swings

3) Trouble falling asleep

4) Hot flashes

5) Night sweats

6) Fatigue and reduced stamina

7) Dry eyes, dry skin, dry vagina, loss of skin's glow

8) Bloating

9) Heart palpitations

[Puberty begins one year earlier than 100 years ago because increased insulin causes an increase in estrogen in females and testosterone in males.]

HOW DO I KNOW IF I AM SECRETING TOO MUCH ESTROGEN?

You will have:

1) Fat around the hips

2) Fat around the butt

3) Fat around the thighs

For men increased estrogen will give them "men boobs"

[The more estrogen you secrete, the more cortisol you secrete.]

ESTROGEN IN FOODS

Chances are when you are eating a hamburger or chicken you are consuming a lot of estrogen. Today, hormones like estrogen are used to fatten up the cows and chickens rapidly. This extra estrogen in our food supply is dangerous because for men it is a major cause of prostate cancer and for women breast cancer.

XENOESTROGENS

Xenoestrogens are estrogen "mimickers" found in our environment. You will find them in plastics, detergents, shampoos, perfumes, moisturizers, fertilizers, pesticides, deodorants and hair spray.

THE THYROID CONNECTION

A woman will often fall through the cracks when it comes to getting a proper diagnosis as far as her thyroid is concerned. The reason for that is most physicians are stuck on "normal testing." So if you go to your doctor with exhaustion and all the tests come back within "normal limits" you will likely be told "You are just depressed. Nothing to worry about." We at the Martin Clinic are keenly aware of what we call "Subclinical Conditions". What do we mean by that? Well you might have "normal tests" for thyroid for example, but you may experience some of the following:

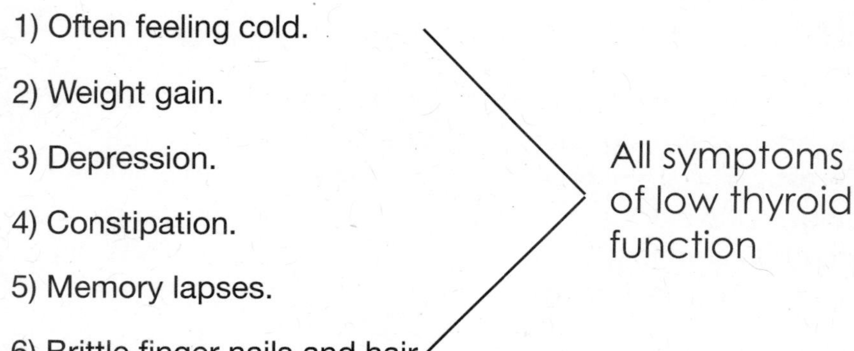

So if one of our patients has these symptoms we go on to test the adrenal glands and especially cortisol levels. We know that there is often a real connection between the adrenals and the thyroid gland.

ANOTHER TRINITY

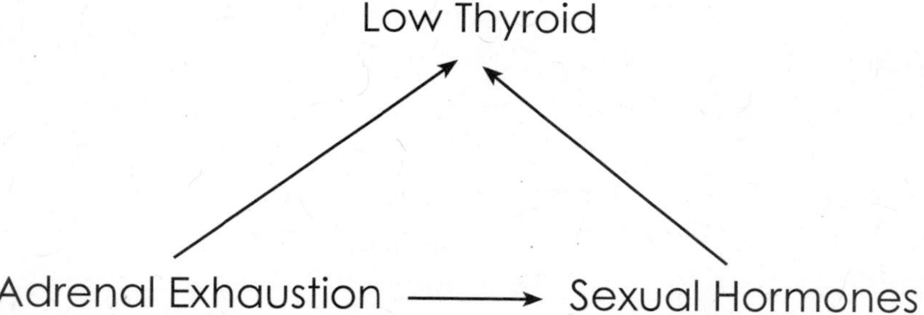

CHAPTER 4
LEAKY GUT

CHAPTER 4

LEAKY GUT

Leaky gut is a major problem in our Western world today. Since the 1970's I have been telling my patients that 80% of all health problems can be traced back to their bowels. Friend, if the plumbing ain't right, then nothing is right.

TALE OF TWO CITIES

In our last book "Energy Robbers" I used the following illustration to explain to leaky gut and a lot of people really liked the analogy. The Americans have two borders, one with Canada and one with Mexico.

CANADIAN BORDER

When Canadians want to go to the United States we are sure put under a lot of scrutiny at the border. Ever since 9/11 it is no fun going across the border. Not only are border guards miserable, but they treat everyone like they are common criminals. You think that Americans would be happy to have Canadians come and spend money in the USA.

MEXICAN BORDER

I could jump in an airplane in Canada and fly over the USA and land in Mexico and then walk into the States. Why? America's southern border has 2000 miles of unprotected border. Mexicans walk into the USA every day to go to work (I don't blame them) with no questions asked.

Now leaky gut is like that. Your bowel is the border between you and you're blood. If you have a healthy bowel your gut will not allow anything into your blood that does not belong (Canadian border). For example when you eat, your food gets digested and broken down from the mouth to the stomach then goes on to the small intestine. In the small intestine, your food is divided into two. What your body doesn't need is sent to the bowel and eventually out of the body. What your body needs (protein, fats, carbs, water, vitamins and minerals) goes across the micro flora in the bowel (small intestine) into the blood stream for transportation to all your body.

Whenever you take an antibiotic or painkillers like Tylenol, Advil, Aleve, Motrin, and Aspirin the normal flora is destroyed in the gut. This causes the gut to be extra permeable (Mexican border). What should have gone out of your body like "crap", fungus, parasites, and toxins seep into your blood stream instead!

Now do you understand what a leaky gut is? The #1 test to diagnose leaky gut is "Live blood microscopy". I really suggest you get the Martin Clinic Bio-Marker testing done-to see if you have leaky gut. This test could save your life!

OTHER CAUSES OF LEAKY GUT

1) The high secretion of cortisol due to stress is a major cause of leaky gut. Cortisol compromises the lining of the gut and prolonged secretion of this serial killer will allow garbage into your blood stream that is highly toxic.

In my research on Chronic Fatigue Syndrome and Fibromyalgia **one hundred percent** of these people had leaky gut. Why? The cause of CFS and Fibromyalgia is Adrenal Exhaustion leading to the over secretion of Cortisol!!

2) Eating a Western diet high in carbs and sugary foods causes the balance of the gut to change drastically, creating an overgrowth of bad bacteria. Artificial preservatives, chemicals and dyes in food also affect the flow of the bowel in a negative way.

3) Low Stomach Acid can cause leaky gut. Healthy levels of stomach acid are needed to break down food. If food from the stomach comes into the bowel undigested, candida has a feeding frenzy.

People have this idea that if they have heartburn or acid indigestion they have too much acidity in their stomachs. But, just the opposite is true. If you do not have enough acidity in your stomach your body will try to produce more thereby causing acid to run up into the esophagus. The worst thing you can do is take Rolaids, Tums, or prescription drugs like Nexium, Tagamet and others. They suppress acidity and give you temporary relief, but in the long run they do absolutely nothing to correct the problem. Taking antacids is like when you hear a knock in the engine and you just turn your radio up louder so you can't hear the knock anymore. The best thing you can do is actually make your stomach more acidic by:

a) Taking a tablespoon of lemon juice or apple cider vinegar

b) Taking digestive enzymes with betaine.

The only place you want to be acidic in all of your body is in the stomach. Everywhere else you want to be alkaline.

Leaky gut is one of the major causes of auto-immune diseases like Lupus and Rheumatoid Arthritis.

If you have low acidity in your stomach-unhealthy bacteria like H-Pylori (ulcer causing) can set up shop and flourish in the stomach or gut.

4) Good Versus Evil - As a Christian I am acutely aware of an invisible battle that takes place in our universe-good versus bad. "We do not wrestle against flesh and blood, but against principalities, against powers, against the rulers of the darkness of this age, against spiritual hosts of wickedness in heavenly places". Ephesians, Chapter 6, verse 12. (NKJV of the Bible).

Well guess what? There is an invisible battle that takes place within us every day-the fight between good and bad bacteria. The modern world has most people trained to think of bacteria as something vile and unhealthy. What you probably don't realize is that most bacteria is actually good for you. Friends, you need trillions of good bacteria in your body in order to keep the bad bacteria at bay.

Good (Friendly)Bacteria (Probiotics);

a) Help digest food properly lessening your risk of food allergies and intolerances.

b) Reduce gas and bloating.

c) Kill fungus and bad bacteria in your gut.

d) Help absorb Vitamin D therefore increasing your immune function.

e) Help to keep your bowels regular and reduce constipation.

f) Act as border guards between your gut and your blood keeping toxins, fungus and parasites out of your blood.

g) Clean up skin problems like acne, eczema and psoriasis.

5) Pesticides and herbicides also kill good bacteria. Let's face it, unless you can afford organic you are going to have to deal with chemicals in our food supply.

6) We over clean!!! The use of antibacterial soaps, wipes and strong cleaners like Mr. Clean, Fantastik and Javex etc. kill the good bacteria along with the bad. One of the reasons we have so many superbugs today like C difficile is that we over clean and overuse antibiotics.

PLEASE DON'T FEED THE BEARS

I come from a small town in Northern Ontario, Canada called Timmins. Where my grandfather David Martin established the Martin Clinic in 1911. Well, whenever I visit Timmins there are two highway signs coming into town that always catch my eye. The

first sign is Timmins the home of Shania Twain'. My only claim to fame is that Shania Twain and I left Timmins at the same time. I guess my other claim to fame is that before she became famous I sat beside her on a plane going from Timmins to Toronto. She was telling me about a new CD she had recorded and that it was going to be released shortly. Well, I guess the rest is history.

The second sign says "Please don't feed the bears". My sister says that there are so many bears in Timmins that they are now buying condos. Every time I see that sign it makes me think of fungus and parasites that gets into a person's bloodstream because of the lack of friendly bacteria. **I always tell my patients when they have candida, fungus or parasites not to feed the bears!!**

PARASITES

> "Because many parasites are thought to be rare, many doctors don't routinely screen for bugs as a cause of fatigue, bloating, nausea. As a result 3 out of 4 women are never diagnosed."
>
> Louise Gittleman pHD

Dr. Oz says, "90% humans will have a problem with parasites in their lifetime."

We at Martin Clinic take parasites quite seriously. The most common parasite we discover is giardia. However, roundworms are often common in women. Parasites can come from cats-(especially kitty litter.) Also if your stomach acid is not strong enough parasites can enter the bowel and make their way to the blood stream. One study suggests that 44% of migraine sufferers have parasites.

***For testing on leaky gut, yeast, fungus, or parasites order the Biomarker Testing Kit from the Marin Clinic www.martinclinic.com**

WHAT FEEDS CANDIDA, FUNGUS AND PARASITES?

<u>THE ANSWER - S.S. AND P. – SUGAR, SWEETS AND PASTRIES</u>

Candida and parasites thrive in blood and tissue when you feed them sugar. So **PLEASE DON'T FEED THE BEARS!**

Sugar in fruit does not feed candida or parasites because the fructose in fruits is surrounded by fiber.

Most yogurts are very poor in probiotics. The reason is because they are not broad spectrum. They also contain sugar which negates the effectiveness of probiotics.

Avoid sugar and starches. They're bad bacteria's favourite meal.
Dr. A. Sears

WHAT ARE THE BEST PROBIOTICS?

The best probiotics are broad spectrum probiotics. Broad spectrum means that they have at least 10 different strains of bacteria. Read the label. Probiotics are like the tribes of Israel, they need to go from Dan to Beersheba. To get complete coverage in your body you need to go from your sinuses to your reproductive organs.

Fruit actually helps to kill candida and parasites because it helps make your body alkaline. Remember, fungus, bad bacteria and parasites thrive in an acidic body.

Another thing to look for in a good probiotic is whether it is "soil based" or not. Soil based probiotics have an advantage because they do not need to be refrigerated. Dairy probiotics lose their potency very quickly.

Research suggests that if we have the right bacteria in our digestive tracts we get fewer calories from our food.
Dr. Mike Moreno
The 17 Day Diet

PREBIOTICS

Prebiotics are to bacteria what fertilizer is to a lawn. Prebiotics have a certain sugar called FOS (fructo-olissacharides) that literally feed good bacteria.

Here are some of the foods that contains prebiotics:

1) Asparagus
2) Maple Syrup-not Aunt Jemina's
3) Honey
4) Garlic, onion and leeks
5) Tomatoes

Did you know that probiotics increase your good cholesterol up to 38%?

The use of antibiotics or intake from commercial dairy and meats tainted with antibiotics destroys friendly bacteria.

> A recent Swedish study found that folks who get plenty of probiotics are significantly less likely to catch colds. If they do get sick their symptoms clear up 2.5 days sooner.

LEAKY GUT AND CHILDHOOD BEHAVIOUR PROBLEMS

Dr. Natasha Campbell-McBride author of "Gut and Psychology Syndrome" has been helping children with behavioural problems for years through diet changes and the balance of internal flora. She learned her methods by curing her autistic son. She notes that early childhood diseases and behavioural problems often occur because the mother's intestinal flora was compromised or destroyed during delivery. The baby inherits it by swallowing the mother's amniotic fluid upon exiting the womb.

Behavioural and physiological disorders such as autism, ADD, ADHD, dyslexia, depression, schizophrenia, bipolar, obsessive compulsive and eating disorders are in epidemic proportions today. If a damaged flora does not affect a child psychologically then it will physically with such disorders as asthma, allergies and eczema.

CHAPTER 5
FOODS THAT LET SERIAL KILLERS GET AWAY WITH MURDER!

CHAPTER 5

FOODS THAT LET SERIAL KILLERS GET AWAY WITH MURDER

CARBS

The #1 serial killer enabler is carbohydrates.

Doctors today are worried about the amount of salt in our diets but we at the Martin Clinic are more worried about the amount of carbohydrates we consume.

The bodies' energy source comes from 3 kinds of foods:

1) Carbohydrates

2) Protein

3) Fat

Carbohydrates are broken down into 10 categories:

1) Fruits and veggies. You also have to understand that fruits and veggies also contain protein and fat but they are mostly carbs.

2) Breads

3) Cereals

4) Pasta

5) Rice

6) Soups, gravies and sauces. Almost all soups are very high in carbs with the exception of beef consommé.

7) Sugar

8) Sweets

9) Pastries- cakes, pies, brownies, cookies, muffins, pizza.

10) Carbohydrate drinks like milk-white or chocolate, fruit

juices and fruit drinks, alcohol (beer, wine, gin, rum, vodka, whiskey, soft drinks, lemonade

* Even yogurts are high in carbohydrates, for example: low fat yogurt with fruit has 43 grams of carbohydrates; plain yogurt with no sugar added has 16.7 grams of carbs.

** Although most nuts are considered high in protein and fat cashews have 18 grams of carbs for a 1 ounce serving; pistachios have 14 grams of carbs for a 2 ounce serving.

YOU KNOW YOU ARE A CARBO-HOLIC WHEN:

"Man shall not live by bread alone but by every word that proceeds out of the mouth of the Lord" Matthew 4:4. I can still remember as a young kid the two smells that got my salivary glands going, even to this day.

Our documented research has shown that 75% of overweight adults identify themselves as "carbohydrate addicts"
Dr. Richard F. Heller
Dr. Rachael F. Heller
"The Carbohydrates Addicts Diet"

Wednesday Night

Every Wednesday my Mom, who was a great cook, would make spaghetti. I remember as a little boy running home as fast as possible just to get a whiff of the spaghetti sauce slow cooking on the stove. Well, guess what I did years later? I married an Italian girl. Yes, not only was she the most beautiful girl in my home town but she was Italian. Her mother taught her to make the best spaghetti sauce and meatballs in the world-yes even better than my mom's. Now we have been married for 39 years and I still never get tired of my wife's cooking or her famous pasta (especially the spaghetti sauce.)

The point is that I could have pasta 7 days a week, 365 days a year. My wife always laughs when she asks" What would you like for supper tonight?" She knows the answer is always the same-spaghetti.

My Ma Tante Delina

In French, to say "my Aunt" you say "Ma Tante". My grandmother's sister-Ma Tante Delina- made homemade "cracked wheat bread" once a week. Wow! I would nearly pass out with excitement as a kid at the thought of eating the bread. Folks, as you can see-I am a carbo-holic. Every time that I read the verse in the bible -Man cannot live by bread alone I chuckle and say to God-well Lord you know me and I am the exception. Just give me bread and spaghetti and I will be completely satisfied.

Friend, can you identify with this story? Then you are a carbo-holic! Now I don't want you to go and join a club and go to meetings but you must, like an alcoholic agree with the diagnosis. You and I have a problem. The problem is carbs. The more carbs you eat the more insulin your pancreas produces and the more cortisol your adrenal glands produce. Before you know it you have a carb belly and carry extra weight.

YOU KNOW YOU ARE A CARBOHOLIC WHEN:

1) You start your day with cereal or toast -6-7 days a week

2) You are prone to overeating

3) You get a burst of energy from eating cookies, soda or chocolate but then experience an energy crash

4) Your skin looks doughy or puffy

5) You have a history of pre-diabetes or diabetes

6) You think a lot about food

7) You favour chocolate to almost anything

8) You favour bread, next to chocolate over almost anything. You can't have a meal without bread

9) You have always struggled with weight

10) You marry an Italian girl for her pasta (just kidding)

11) You become light-headed and irritable if you miss a meal

*12) You have what used to be called a "beer belly"-it really is a "carb belly"

Friends you need carbs in your diet, especially good carbs. The best carbs are of course fruit and vegetables. We almost completely separate fruits and veggies from the carbohydrate list because they contain fiber. *HAVE YOU NOTICED HOW MANY CHILDREN HAVE CARB-BELLIES? NOW IT IS AN EPIDEMIC!*

[Fiber also prevents most fat in our foods from being absorbed.]

Fiber makes fruits and vegetables almost protein-like because it diminishes the amount of insulin needed to convert them to a simple sugar.

Some fruits and vegetables that should be limited in a low carb eating plan are the following:

Vegetables	Fruit and Juices
Beans Chickpeas Potatoes Peas Corn	Dried Fruit, Sweetened applesauce, Bananas, Figs, Grape juice, Sweetened juices, Mangos, Canned peaches, pears or pineapple, Pineapple juice

SUGAR, SWEETS AND PASTRIES

I want to spend extra time writing about these 3 particular carbs: sugar, sweets and pastries. These 3 foods, more than anything else have allowed the Serial Killers, cortisol and insulin to run wild and wreak havoc in our society today.

Jorge Cruise (not Tom) in his book "The Belly Fat Cure" suggests that we now consume 60% more sweets and sugar than in our mom's time. In the 1970's when I graduated, the average North American was consuming 40 pounds of sugar a year now it is around 170 pounds of sugar a year.

> Sugar, sweets and pastries should be charged as co-conspirators with cortisol and insulin.

Sugar is in almost everything today. If you shop in the middle isle of your grocery store and look at the label you will be shocked. Sugar is added to:

1) Almost all breads

2) Almost all cereals including oatmeal

3) Infant formula

4) Almost all soups and sauces

5) Cookies, crackers

6) Fruit juice

7) Almost all yogurts

8) Dips

9) Ketchup, relish

10) Puddings

11) All deserts

"At any given time we have 100-10,000 cancer cells in our bodies, therefore we should avoid sugar as much as possible."
Dr. Shukla

*Read the ingredients and anything with fructose, high fructose corn syrup or cane sugar should be avoided.

DOC - WHAT ABOUT THE SUGAR FOUND IN FRUIT?

God meant for us to eat fructose surrounded by fiber. That is why fruits are so good for you. When you take the fiber away from the fruit then the fructose will spike your insulin and blood sugar rapidly. Therefore you must make juices and smoothies with freshly squeezed or blended berries and drinking all of the pulp with it.

Recent Japanese studies found that women who consumed the most carbs were more likely to be depressed.

[Cancer cells have 8 times more receptors for sugar than healthy cells!]

SUGAR AND CANCER

Cancer cells depend more heavily on glycolysis - a process that breaks down sugar for energy according to Gerald Krystal PhD. University of British Columbia.

Depriving the body of carbs especially sugar and sweets allows normal cells to live off fat and cancer cells to die!!!

[When your blood sugar spikes after a high carb meal your cancer cells have a feast.]

Otto Warburg as early as 1931 suggested that cancer cells need sugar to proliferate.

Dr. Simincini, an Italian Oncologist, suggests that all cancers are fungus based and fungus needs sugar to thrive.

DAIRY AND GLUTEN

Almost every day I have patients coming in to our office with intolerances to dairy or gluten or both. I mean every second person today has some kind of food intolerance. Here are symptoms of other food intolerance. You could be SUGAR INTOLERANT if you have three or more of the following symptoms:

1) Brain fog
2) Irritability
3) Moody
4) Headaches
5) Joint pain and muscle aches
6) Sleeplessness
7) Cravings for sweets
8) Worsening of PMS
9) Stomach gurgling
10) Nausea

> Sugar and high fructose are loaded with empty calories. They also spike your blood sugar making you even hungrier. During digestion sugar and syrup are sent to the liver which tells your body to turn them into fat.

If you have 3 or more of these symptoms on a regular basis you have developed sugar/simple carb intolerance.

CASE HISTORY

A 45 year old man (I will call him George) entered our clinic for help to lose weight. He was at least 60-80 pounds overweight. Upon questioning he admitted that he was a carbo-holic. He was very moody with his wife and kids and had a short fuse. He noticed that he often snapped at his wife and children for the littlest of things. He said that he wasn't always like this and he seemed to have had a change in personality in the last few years.

He often indulged in binge eating especially ice cream and chocolate, and he experienced headaches every other day. He had sleep apnea and a lot of joint pain and muscle aches.

Our testing revealed very high levels of insulin and cortisol. We put him on the Serial Killer Diet with a severe limit on his sugar and simple carb intake. The changes in him were dramatic. Within a week he noticed a higher level of energy and even his wife commented on his new pleasant demeanour.

CHAPTER 6

FAT:

IS NOT THE NEW BOGEYMAN

CHAPTER 6

FAT IS NOT THE NEW BOGEYMAN

Reducing fat has been the cornerstone of dietary guidelines for years. This is not based on science but rather a lie. Remember, if you say a lie long enough it will become a new truth.

FOR EXAMPLE

1) EVOLUTION

When I was a kid evolutionary teaching was just getting started as a science. The old pictures of a monkey walking on all fours then developing to an upright ape and then to a caveman and then to modern man was starting to take root as acceptable teaching in public and even some Catholic schools. If scientists said that it was true, well then it must be. See how a lie gets started. Here we are in 2011 and if you even bring up creation in a discussion you are considered a moron.

In Canada, our Prime Minister-Steven Harper told all of his potential MP's (Members of Parliament) to keep quiet about their religious beliefs otherwise they would never get elected. This happened after the former leader of Canada's conservative party-Stockwell Day was ridiculed by the media for believing in creation. The media did the same to George W. Bush. Well folks, I am a scientist and an unapologetic creationist!! Look at the world around you. Look at the heavens with a telescope and then study the human body. Tell me with a straight face that there is no God, All the precision and beauty of the universe and the marvels of the human body just happened by chance. COME ON NOW! I refuse to be led by the masses. I don't care if the vast majority believes in evolution-I don't buy it. Science demands observation, measurement and repetition. Sorry folks, evolutionary teaching does not pass the smell test. But, like I said, if you say something long enough the vast majority of people will believe that it is true.

2) GLOBAL WARMING

"...say a lie long enough and you will believe it."

Here is another lie. Left wing people like Al Gore started this nonsense about global warming and that it is man-made. Tree huggers and the like take it hook, line and sinker. Well folks, I don't buy it. I am not convinced by the science which has proven to be shoddy at best. Like I said-say a lie long enough and you will believe it.

3) STATIN DRUGS

Years ago the drug companies came up with a plan to sell more drugs. I would have loved to have been a fly on the wall listening to marketing genius' on how they could make statin drugs (cholesterol lowering medication like Lipitor, Crestor, Zocor etc.) sell like gangbusters. Well folks, they succeeded. In the early 1990's the statins were selling about #100 on the drug list of best sellers. Today they are #1 and the hits just keep on coming!!!

The drug companies have convinced the medical profession that prescription statin drugs are preventative. I mean who does not want prevention?

Drug companies are in the business of selling drugs. Some of them are essential but for the most part they have succeeded in duping the medical community to give out statins like candies. Here is how Big Pharma has accomplished this task:

1) Convince the public and doctors that cholesterol is a disease.

2) Get the medical profession to change what is a normal cholesterol reading to make them abnormal.

3) Convince the public and doctors that eggs have cholesterol

and therefore should be avoided.

4) Convince the diabetic associations to adopt policies that the recommended diabetic treatment plan should be to start on cholesterol lowering medications (even if their cholesterol is normal).

5) Spend millions of dollars in advertising to the public and marketing to doctors on the advantages of cholesterol medications.

6) Minimize the criticism of the side effects of statins. Fudge the numbers on research and convince the FDA and Health Canada that cholesterol medication is safe. Limit the research on Omega 3 and dietary changes (like adding 40 grams of fiber a day) as being as effective on lowering bad cholesterol as statin drugs with no side effects.

7) Convince the medical profession that prescription statin drugs is preventative. I mean who does not want prevention?

8) I have to give the drug companies credit. They have been an enormous success. They have made billions of dollars a year in revenues and the public and doctors have bought it big time.

4) THE SUN IS THE BAD GUY!

Again let's give credit where credit is due. The makers of sun screen lotion and dermatologists started a trend in the 80's to lower skin cancer and blame the sun. Today parents lather up their kids with sun block. A weather forecast lets us know about the dangers of UV radiation. Say a lie long enough and people will believe.

Johnson and Johnson (a family company) and others have so convinced the public that the sun is responsible for the vast majority of new skin cancers today. Friends, here is a fact for every person who dies from melanoma (skin cancer), 250 people die from a lack of Vitamin D. Now do not go out and tell everyone that Dr. Martin says that you can get as much sun as you want and that there is no consequence to burning. However, today the vast majority of people in North America are surprisingly deficient in Vitamin D because the sun is now the bad guy. Once again the public has now been fooled.

SUNSCREENS AND SKIN CANCER

This is my opinion-the overuse of sunblocks and sunscreens you are using are the major cause of skin cancer. By the way, the best sunscreen you can use is taking antioxidants and using either vitamin E oil or ReVera (a natural sunscreen formulated by the Martin Clinic).

5) EGGS

As a clinical nutritionist I almost went crazy in the 1980's when people started believing the lie about how eggs are bad for you. Doctors who know so little about nutrition believed the lie and started telling all of their patients to avoid eggs like the plague. Eggs have cholesterol therefore they must be bad for you. What poor science! Actually eggs are good for your heart. The liver makes 85% of your cholesterol. Eggs are such a good source of protein they will lower your cholesterol! Remember blaming cholesterol for heart disease is like blaming the police for crime just because they are at the scene of the crime.

Cholesterol is not the bad guy. Inflammation, free radicals and an acidic pH are the bad guys in heart disease. Cholesterol will never stick to healthy blood vessels. Cholesterol only sticks to blood vessels that are damaged by inflammation, free radicals and low pH (acidic).

In my last book "Energy Robbers" I mention that the #1 food one can eat to stimulate their energy is eggs. Friends, most people have believed another lie. How easily we are fooled.

God gave you a brain-use it!! Just because doctors say it or it is on the news, you don't have to believe it. Investigate and do your own thinking. Don't have the herd mentality or follow the pied piper – THINK!!

6) BUTTER

Remember in the 80"s? "They" said no more butter. What nonsense!!! Then "they" said let's have a substitute for butter- margarine. Never mind that margarine is an artificial food. "So good it tastes like butter" The whole Western world went hook, line and sinker. People by the millions were avoiding butter like it was a dangerous food. Again dieticians, doctors and the general public followed the pied piper and believed another lie.

NOW BACK TO FAT!

THE ONLY BAD FAT IS TRANSFAT!!!!

DON'T SKIMP ON FAT

"Saturated fat is not doing anything when it comes to cardiovascular risk. What is more crucial is to look at what people are replacing it with." Dr. Promod Khosla, Associate Professor of Nutrition and Food Science, Wayne State University.

> "No significant evidence that dietary fat is associated with the increased risk of coronary heart disease"
> Dr. Ronald Krauss American Journal of Clinical Nutrition

If we replace fat with carbs especially refined carbs like breads, bagels, donuts and sugary cereals etc. we increase our risk of cardiovascular disease.

YOUR BRAIN AND FAT

If someone calls you fathead, do not get insulted. Your brain is made up of 60% fat. You absolutely need fat for your brain to function properly.

In my practice I warn my patients about living and eating a fat free lifestyle. If you do not get enough fat in your diet your brain is one of the first organs to suffer.

ALZHEIMERS AND INSULIN

A high insulin level caused by insulin resistance due to a high carbohydrate diet is one of the worst things you can do for your brain function. Here is what is commonly found with people who have Alzheimers or dementia.

1) There is a build-up of plaque in the arteries. Now once again most doctors have an idea that if you have plaque build-up it is because you have consumed too much fat and cholesterol in your diet. But remember, **THE CULPRIT IS INFLAMMATION - NOT FAT!**

INFLAMMATION is caused by several factors:

1) High levels of insulin in the blood
2) High levels of cortisol in the blood

>The Serial Killers

3) Our toxic environment

4) Inflammatory diet-high S, S and P (sweets, sugar and pastries)

5) Auto-immune disorders such as Lupus, MS, Chronic Fatigue and Fibromyalgia

6) Acidic pH

7) Low Omega 3 levels in the blood

TRANS-FATS (THE ONLY REAL BAD FAT)

Trans-fats in general come from hydrogenated soybean oil. Trans-fats have long been associated with making bad cholesterol. Research going back as far as 1982 indicates that trans-fats found in partially hydrogenated vegetable oil can fundamentally alter how the body metabolizes fat in general.

Kylie Kavanaugh of Wake Forest, University School of Medicine, fed monkeys trans-fats and they gained 33% more abdominal fat than monkeys fed olive oil (monounsaturated fat).

Food manufacturers have been very reluctant to stop using trans-fats in their foods because it is so cheap and increases a products shelf life!

The FDA and Health Canada guidelines were meant to weed out trans fats. "These guidelines have been a disappointment because manufacturers can actually claim that a food is trans-fat free as long as it contains less than 500mg per serving" says Michel D Ozner, MD; Chairman of the American Heart Association.

This is disturbing because according to the USDA 4,200 foods on the American market still contain trans-fats including 40% of all prepared foods such as: 1) Desserts, 2) Spreads, 3) Baking Mixes, 4) Chips, 5) Cereals 6) Frozen Foods

Food manufacturers have been very reluctant to stop using trans-fats in their foods because it is so cheap and increases a products shelf life!

TRANS-FATS ARE THE REAL BOGEYMAN- WHY?

1) They can prematurely age your brain by 19 years.

2) They can increase a woman's heart disease risk by 47%.

3) They weaken the immune system.

4) They increase your cancer risk.

5) They reduce the quality of milk in nursing mothers.

6) They are a huge factor in increasing your obesity risk.

In a 10 year study of 667 elderly men, Dutch researchers found that a high intake of trans-fats was associated with a 28% increased risk of coronary heart disease.

> National Academy of Science estimates that trans-fats were to blame for up to 50,000 US deaths a year.

GOOD FATS

1) Coconut Oil

2) Extra Virgin Olive oil

3) Macadamia Nut Oil

4) Fish Oil

5) Hemp Seed Oil

6) Flax Seeds

> Barry Sears the author of "Toxic Fat" says "Fish oil reduces cellular inflammation, one of the key triggers of body fat formation. Plus it shuts down your brain's production of hunger promoting hormones for up to 6 hours and activates your liver's fat burning genes".

COCONUT OIL

Some of the many health and healing benefits of high quality, unrefined, natural coconut oil are as follows:

♥ Increases immunity

♥ Decreases inflammation

♥ Boosts energy

♥Improves nutrient absorption

♥Increases metabolism

♥Assists in the treatment of yeast infections

♥Protects and moisturizes skin

♥Helps protect the liver

♥Assists in weight loss

♥Coconut oil has natural anti-oxidants

♥Coconut oil is rich in fatty acids that have natural antiviral and antibacterial properties. It contains Monolaurin which is the same anti-microbial agent found in a human mother's milk.

Coconut oil is saturated oil BUT, not all saturated fats are alike and current research shows that the fatty acids in coconut oil, the medium chain triglycerides, do not raise serum cholesterol or contribute to heart disease. This is the oil that tastes like coconuts which is fine for salads however, for stir frying there is the tasteless coconut oil.

Extra Virgin Olive Oil is a high chain fatty acid and can develop trans-fats at high temperatures. Its many benefits are:

1) Anti-inflammatory

2) Can help decrease heart disease

3) Anti-oxidant

4) 75% oleic acid (Omega 9)

OLIVE OIL- it contains oleic acid-a micronutrient that helps stop insulin production

5) Decreases blood pressure

6) Anti-cancer

7) Decreases platelet aggregation (naturally thins the blood)

8) Bone health benefits

9) Cognitive benefits

Olive oil and nuts in diet control heart disease better than dangerous drug therapies. Natural news.com Sept.7/11

Macadamia Nut Oil can be used in a low carbohydrate based diet. As the oil is derived from nuts, there are several good points for using it. Macadamia Nut oil consists of 80 % mono-saturated fats. Moreover, the oil has no trans-fatty acids and the rate of saturated fat is comparatively low. So, it is the best way of enhancing heart's health. For sugar regulation and controlling diabetes, Macadamia Nut oil is highly effective. For cooking purposes this oil is exceedingly important because it is resistant to chemical alteration which takes place when cooked at high temperatures. This makes Macadamia Nut oil one of the healthiest oils. Macadamia oil owes its stability mostly to its extremely low omega-6 fatty acid content (the lowest of all traditional cooking oils, next to coconut oil), its high monounsaturated fatty acid content and a decent portion of saturated fat (around 16%, which is good for a nut oil). Omega-6 linoleic acid is the most unstable, so having almost none of it makes macadamia oil superior to most. Macadamia oil also contains varying amounts of antioxidants.

*People eating the lowest levels of fat in their diets had the highest insulin levels according to a recent study done in Quebec, Canada.

FISH OIL

1) Prevents blood clots

2) Lowers bad cholesterol

3) Reduces the risk of heart attack

4) Reduces your risk of Alzheimer's and dementia

5) Reduces your risk of depression

6) Aids in the treatment of inflammation (arthritis, fibromyalgia, ADD, ADHD)

7) Helps in fat loss

WHAT!! FAT CAN HELP YOU LOSE WEIGHT???!

In the last several years "low fat" or "0% fat" has monopolized the food shelves in our grocery stores. From crackers to yogurt to even ice cream, food manufactures have tried to fool the public with this deception. Did you know that eating a low fat diet will keep your insulin levels high? Choosing olive oil, avocados, peanut butter (no sugar added) and nuts actually prompt the body to produce more Adinopectin –a sugar hormone that accelerates the metabolism, decreases insulin and reduces inflammation.

> In 2009, obese patients who followed a low fat diet for several months actually lost NO FAT around their belly at all.

SATURATED FAT

Saturated fat can actually reduce depression according to a study in the Journal of Clinical Investigation. Great sources of saturated fat are coconut oil, butter, ground beef, dark chocolate, salmon and eggs.

THE ONLY MILK I RECOMMEND

I understand that buying whole milk that is unpasteurized is almost impossible to get in North America. I believe that milk today is a major cause of asthma, acne, allergies, diabetes and many other conditions. I always say to my patients that if you have a cow in the back yard then go for it-drink milk. If you don't, then avoid it as much as possible.

The problem with today's milk is that:

1) It is high in carbohydrates and converts to sugar quickly.

2) High heat pasteurization denatures the milk causing severe intolerances to lactose (milk sugar) and casein (milk protein).

> 2/3 of the population has some kind of intolerance to milk.

3) If you have to drink milk, then drink the milk that has the highest concentration of fat. I go crazy when I see people drinking "skim milk or 1% milk. This type of milk causes the most problems, because it is the furthest from its purest form.

Full fat dairy milk is rich in (CLA) conjugated linoleic acid. According to research at California's Miramar University in San Diego, daily intake of this essential fatty acid hinders production of lipoprotein-lipase, an enzyme involved in the formation and maintenance of body fat stores. This helps women to shed up to 22% more of body fat in 6 months.

> "When you take all the fat out of milk you're left with too high a concentration of natural sugars which interacts like candy with insulin."
> Dr. Oz Time Magazine, Sept. 12/11

Therefore adding healthy fats like olive oil, flax seeds and hemp seed oil to your diet will dramatically lower insulin function. When insulin is lower you burn more fat for energy.

WHY YOUR BODY NEEDS SATURATED FAT AND CHOLESTEROL?

1) Fifty percent of your cell's walls are made up of saturated fat.

2) The fat around your heart is made up of saturated fat.

3) Sixty percent of the brain is fat. Fat free brains are Alzheimer's and Dementia brains.

4) Medium chain fatty acids like those found in coconut oil are antifungal and are important for thyroid function.

5) Cholesterol is a precursor to Vitamin D and major hormones like estrogen, sex hormones and testosterone.

6) Fat plays a vital role in the health of our bones. For example, calcium needs saturated fat for it to be absorbed.

7) Fat enhances the immune system.

8) Fat acts as a natural antidepressant by enhancing serotonin receptors. Decreased cholesterol is associated with violent behaviour, depression and suicidal tendencies.

9) The more saturated fat one consumes, the more the body retains long chain Omega 3. This is critically important for cardiovascular health.

10) Cholesterol protects the liver from alcohol and prescription drug damage.

OTHER FOODS THAT HELP TRACK DOWN SERIAL KILLERS

PROTEIN GETS A BAD RAP

How many people do I know that eat very little protein because they thought it was bad for them. They avoid meat, eggs, cheese like the plague. Protein is needed for every body function and because of its role in muscle and tissue structure and function including the skin, cartilage, blood, hair, nails, organs and hormones. Next to water, protein is the most important part of a healthy diet.

USES OF PROTEIN

1) Protein stabilizes blood sugar

2) Protein helps with the feeling of fullness thus helping to suppress appetite. I tell my patients if they are hungry all day long they are not eating enough protein.

3) Protein boosts your metabolic rate which is how you burn calories.

4) Protein helps to preserve muscle. A lot of people who lose weight don't look good because they have lost muscle with their weight loss. It is better to lose water and fat and keep the muscle.

5) Protein does not increase the risk of heart disease according to Harvard University

People eating the most protein lost 40% less muscle in the elderly. American Journal of Clinical Nutrition

People on a high protein, low carb diet averaged 10 times greater decrease in triglycerides (blood fats) than those on a low fat diet. Nutrition Reporter, Sept. 2008

Eating eggs on a low carb diet boosts "good" cholesterol. Nutrition Reporter, March, 2008

EAT YOUR STEAK AND EGGS – WHY I LOVE THEM!

The #1 food to reduce insulin and cortisol is eggs. Around 20 years ago dieticians and physicians decided that cholesterol in eggs was translating to artery-clogging cholesterol in the blood. Therefore eggs were put on the no-no list.

Most people that I see who have trouble losing weight have sluggish metabolisms. Remember, muscle is the body's principle fat burning tissue. Protein requires high energy to metabolize to get a high thermogenic effect. The energy required is 3 times higher than carbohydrates or fat. When eating protein in combination with exercise, fat will burn at a higher rate.

> More protein and less carbs reduce appetite and weight.
> Nutrition Reporter, Feb. 2006

> Eating eggs for breakfast is better than bagels for weight loss and leaves you less hungry.
> Nutrition Reporter, Jan. 2009

PROTEIN AND GLUCAGON

Protein increases glucagon which counter balances the effect of insulin. Glucagon, a hormone secreted by the pancreas, raises blood glucose levels. Its effect is opposite that of insulin, which lowers blood glucose levels.

The pancreas releases glucagon when blood sugar (glucose) levels fall too low.

Glucagon causes the liver to convert stored glycogen into glucose, which is released into the bloodstream and raises blood glucose levels. Most people have about 60-90 % of liver glucagon which can be used up during strenuous exercise. Glucagon lowers cholesterol production.

High blood glucose levels stimulate the release of insulin.

Insulin allows glucose to be taken up and used by insulin-dependent tissues. This is needed for the breakdown of fat and protein for energy. Thus, glucagon and insulin are part of a feedback system that keeps blood glucose levels at a stable level.

Glucagon is a mild diuretic because it signals the kidney to release water which is good for weight loss but you must watch for dehydration.

FIBER

Fiber, (or roughage), is the indigestible part of a plant.

FIBER FACTS:

1) Reduces blood sugar

2) Reduces insulin levels

3) Our bodies need 30-40 grams daily of fiber, we are only getting 10-20 grams a day.

4) Fiber slows down the glycemic response, therefore the whole fructose in fruit does not disrupt your insulin level.

5) Fiber reduces the risk of diverticulitis caused by eating too many processed foods.

THREE TYPES OF FIBER

Fiber is either soluble or insoluble.

1) Insoluble fiber does not dissolve in water and helps move food through the lower digestive tract. Whole wheat, grains and nuts are good sources of insoluble fiber.

2) Soluble fiber absorbs water like a sponge, making a gel like mass and is beneficial for lowering cholesterol levels and maintaining steady blood sugar levels. Good examples of soluble fiber are oat bran, bananas, legumes, peas, lentils and broccoli.

3) Fermentable fiber in foods isn't digested, but as it passes through your system it provides food sources for helpful bacteria, or probiotics to flourish. Fermentable fiber in your diet not only makes your digestive system healthier, but may boost your immune system. An example is the pectin in apples.

PART 2

SERIAL KILLER DIET

CHAPTER 7

INTRODUCTION TO THE SERIAL KILLER DIET

CHAPTER 7

THE SERIAL KILLER DIET - PHASE 1

TESTIMONIALS FROM A THIRTY PEOPLE PILOT STUDY

Several months ago 30 volunteers entered a pilot study on the Serial Killer Diet. Fifteen of these were suffering from Chronic Fatigue Syndrome and Fibromyalgia. All were put on the Serial Killer Diet which is a high fat, low carbohydrate eating plan. All of the thirty were tested for cortisol and insulin and their results were all high.

Before we go into the actual eating plan, let me give you a few quotes from some of the thirty who entered the study after a few weeks on the Serial Killer Diet plan.

– "Just wanted to say it's been over 2 weeks since I started the Serial Killer Diet and I am beginning to feel great. I am happier and my energy is returning. I even sleep better."

– Dr. Martin, "First off let me thank you for helping me change my life! I thought that I was doomed to feel the way I was feeling forever. I now feel so much better physically and emotionally!"

– "Things are going well for the both of us. My husband is feeling much better and he has noticed that his constant bloating has gone. He also noticed that the shortness of breath has gone away and he does not need his puffer and his snoring has decreased. As for myself I am down 10 pounds and feeling much better. We would like to just thank you for everything. I have been recommending your clinic to everyone I know."

– "The day I volunteered for the Serial Killer Diet was the best day of my life. I have lost 7 inches in just 4 weeks and more importantly-feel great-I've got my life back."

– "Over the years I have tried so many diets and just became more frustrated as the scale might show some weight loss but I still had the "pot belly." After one week on the Serial Killer Diet I lost 2 inches on my waist, then 4 inches after 2 weeks. Thank you Dr. Martin."

– "I am on day 4 and have lost 4.2 pounds and can see my knees without bending forward for the first time in years."

THE MANY BENEFITS OF THE SERIAL KILLER DIET

1) Your body burns fat as a primary source of fuel.

2) People very often eat much less on the Serial Killer Diet. Why? When you eat a high fat diet it will strongly blunt hunger feelings.

3) This high fat, low carb diet also naturally spares lean muscle mass far more than normal diets. Sparing lean muscle mass is incredibly important to dieters, as it helps keep your metabolism from slowing down.

4) The first fat to go is the "Belly fat" or a better word for this is "carb belly." So remember to measure your waist around your belly button-the first morning that you start this program.

5) High energy-The Serial Killer diet was foremost formulated to lower cortisol and insulin secretion in the body. As it has been stated in the first half of the book these two hormones will suck the life out of you. Once you start on this diet your energy levels will increase substantially.

FAT DOES NOT MAKE YOU FAT – SUGAR DOES!

I know it is going to take a major shift in your thinking to accept that a high fat diet is actually good for you. I hope that we have made our case that the problem in this unhealthy world is not fat but carbs.

OIL, OIL, OIL

Think of the fat that you are about to eat as oil. Your body needs oil to operate. Your brain needs oil to function properly. Your joints need oil to move properly. Your skin needs oil to look young and vibrant.

"Olive oil and nuts (healthy fat) in diet control heart disease better than dangerous drug therapies."
Atherosclerosis Journal Sept. /2011

75% of processed foods contain genetically modified products such as canola, soybean or corn products.

Everything you heard about fat is just not true!!

The only bad fats are trans fats. They are found in processed foods.

SERIAL KILLER DIET - PHASE 1

SUNDAY TO FRIDAY - CONSUME 30 GRAMS OR LESS OF CARBS PER DAY

REWARD DAYS -EAT YOUR CARBS FROM FRIDAY EVENING TO SUNDAY MORNING

REMEMBER!!!

*NO COUNTING CALORIES

*MUST EAT HIGH FAT FOODS

*THROW AWAY THE SCALE

*MUST TAKE REWARD DAYS

INTRODUCTION TO SERIAL KILLER DIET

David Martin started the Martin Clinic in Timmins, Ontario in 1911. One thing for sure his practice was much different than mine in 2011, exactly 100 years later. I've seen pictures in these early days and there was not one obese patient! As a matter of fact Edward S. Cutis took 177,000 pictures in 1911 and it is stunning to see thin and vibrant people in every picture. One hundred years ago a fat person would be in a circus.

People then had a simple diet comprised mainly of high fat, high protein and fiber. They ate eggs, meat, butter, cream, vegetables and fruits in season.

Today, our society is increasingly debilitated by obesity, diabetes, pre-diabetes, digestive disorders, inflammatory diseases and circulatory diseases. Why? The simple reason is that we have gotten away from our ancestors diet and shifted to a very high carbohydrate way of eating. From pizza, to white bread, Kraft dinner, sugary drinks we are now consuming 10 times more carbohydrates than 100 years ago.

Between now and 2030 the cost of treating cancer, diabetes, heart disease, lung disease and mental health disorders will top 47 trillion dollars according to a report released by the World Economic Forum (WEF). Friends, if this happens the global economy will collapse.

So, the Martin Clinic has a solution. Our new eating plan called "The Serial Killer Diet". This new way of eating if implemented will allow you as an individual to take control of your health. Don't be a statistic no matter what the status of your health is currently.

Remember, you get brand new blood every 4 months. You get a whole new body every seven years. However, if you make no changes in your diet you will succumb to the degenerative diseases that plague North Americans today.

THE SERIAL KILLER DIET

PHASE 1

Sunday morning to Friday evening you consume 30 grams of carbohydrates or less per day. Your "reward" or "cheat" day starts Friday evening at 6 pm to Sunday morning.

THE KEY-KETOSIS

Most people have approximately 3 days of carbohydrates to burn. This is the #1 reason our society struggles with low energy and obesity. As long as a person eats a high amount of carbs on a daily basis they will never get to burn fat. Therefore the Serial Killer Diet forces one to burn fat. To accomplish this you must restrict carbs and increase fat and protein.

The Serial Killer Diet will send you into ketosis. Ketosis simply means:

YOU HAVE ONLY FAT TO BURN!!

Atkins was no dummy!! You might be thinking that this diet is a version of the Atkins diet. Dr. Atkins was often maligned by so-called specialists. First of all Dr. Atkins was a cardiologist. He understood that carbs were the culprit in our society. The problem with the Atkins diet is that most people would get original success for a month or two, but eating this way was too boring and hard to maintain.

THE SERIAL KILLER DIET IS NOT THE ATKINS DIET!!

First of all it is important to eat carbs. The Serial Killer Diet allows you as many carbs as you like on "Reward Days." These reward days will keep you motivated to stay on the program.

THE SERIAL KILLER DIET IS MEANT TO BE FOREVER

We at the Martin clinic want you to stay on this program forever. It is a healthy way to eat. You will probably avoid diabetes with this style of eating. You will help keep cortisol and insulin at bay. You will never have to avoid your favourite foods. Your reward days allow you to enjoy desserts, pasta, bread and even ice cream.

THE IMPORTANCE OF REWARD DAYS

I can't emphasize enough the importance of Reward days. In my 38 years of experience in practice I know one thing about the human personality. We are a people of rewards. When I read the bible I realize that God is a God of rewards. If you trust in His Son the Lord Jesus Christ and believe in His sacrificial death and His resurrection God give you eternal life!! Talk about a reward.

THE SERIAL KILLER DIET ONLY WORKS IF YOU TAKE YOUR REWARD DAYS AND ENJOY THEM.

WHY THE REWARD DAYS?

1) You get to enjoy your favourite carbohydrate like bread, pasta, Chinese food, desserts, etc.

2) You will stick to the program for the long term.

3) Long term ketosis is not sustainable. Your body was not meant to burn only fat. <u>The Serial Killer Diet works because you get to cheat.</u>

4) Most of the 30 people in the pilot study loved the reward days but all were happy to get back to low carb eating on Sunday morning.

SERIAL KILLER DIET - PHASE 2

SUNDAY MORNING TO FRIDAY EVENING 6PM

-100-150g/ **CARBS** DAILY (ADD FRUITS AND VEGGIES)

-HIGH FAT

-HIGH PROTEIN

-REWARD DAYS – FRIDAY 6PM TO SUNDAY MORNING

*PHASE 2 MAINTENANCE MEANT TO LAST A LIFETIME!

PHASE 2 IS TO BE STARTED WHEN YOU HAVE ACHIEVED YOUR DESIRED GOALS OF:

1) HIGH ENERGY

2) BETTER CONCENTRATION

3) FAT LOSS

**PHASE 2 IS NO LONGER KETOSIS THEREFORE YOU WILL NOT BE BURNING ONLY FAT.

CHAPTER 8

QUESTION

&

ANSWERS

QUESTIONS AND ANSWERS

These are some of the examples of questions we received from those involved in our pilot study:

Q – IS KETOSIS DANGEROUS?

A – Absolutely not! Temporary ketosis, we argue is actually good for you. Remember, during this time you will only be burning fat.

Q – HOW DO I KNOW IF I AM INTO KETOSIS?

A – The only way to tell for sure is to test the urine for ketones. You can purchase the urine strips at a pharmacy or from the Martin Clinic. www.martin clinic.com or 1-866-660-6607. However, if you are on a low carb intake (30 grams or less per day) you will be into ketosis.

Q – DO I NEED A DOCTOR TO SUPERVISE THIS DIET?

A – We at Martin clinic always recommend you discuss any program concerning you're eating with your health care provider. However, the program is pretty straight forward. The idea behind The Serial Killer Diet is to decrease carbohydrate intake and up your healthy fat intake.

Q – DR. MARTIN YOU HAVE BEEN PREACHING THE VIRTUES OF FRUITS AND VEGGIES FOR YEARS NOW. WHY THE SUDDEN CHANGE?

A – Well, understand this program was originally developed for people who were exhausted. They have high levels of cortisol and insulin. In order to kick start the program we have to restrict fruits and some vegetables in Phase One. We actually encourage eating as many fruits and veggies on Reward days. Phase Two has all the fruits and veggies you want at all times.

Q – CAN I SPEED UP THE PROCESS OF KETOSIS?

A – Ketosis is the result of being in the fat burning mode. That being said, there is no benefit to being in more ketosis or less ketosis. It is like being pregnant. You either are or you are not! The idea of Reward Days is to replenish the glycogen (stored glucose) in the muscles.

Q – WHAT ABOUT EXERCISE? YOU HAVE HARDLY MENTIONED IT.

A – Anyone who knows us at the Martin clinic will confirm that we are big time proponents of exercise. If we could bottle exercise it would be the #1 vitamin you could take. However, fat loss is 90% diet and 10% exercise. Exercise will no doubt help in reducing insulin and cortisol. Did you know it is impossible to exercise and be stressed at the same time? By the way, it is impossible to reshape the body without weight training!

Q – WHY AM I FEELING FULL YET I SEEM TO BE TAKING IN MUCH LESS CALORIES?

A – Simply because you are consuming much more fat. Increased fat will give you a feeling of fullness. Protein is also very good for curbing the appetite. On The Serial Killer Diet you will be eating much more fat and protein.

Q – WHAT VITAMINS AND MINERALS SHOULD I BE TAKING?

A – It is important to increase your Magnesium intake to 400mg.-1000mg/per day. We also recommend 200-400mg. of potassium.

Q –WHY DO I NEED LOTS OF WATER?

A – Remember, carbs are like sponges. They retain water. Therefore on a low carbohydrate diet you need a lot more water.

We recommend making water your #1 drink. Get away from drinking juices (all carbs) and sodas.

Think of your brain as a grid full of electrical wires. Do you know where we in Ontario get a lot of our power? Your right-Niagara Falls. When you want to see the power of water just think of Niagara Falls. Most headaches come from a lack of water. People are very dry today. The vast majority of people drink very little water.

Q –HOW MUCH WATER SHOULD I DRINK?

A – The minimum amount during Phase 1 would be 64 ounces or 2 litres of water daily. If you work out and sweat easily or are on prescription drugs you will need even more.

Q –WHAT IS THE BEST WATER TO DRINK?

A – Natural spring water is best because it is full of minerals. The more minerals you have in water the more alkaline the water will be. Keep in mind that most of the people we test at The Martin Clinic have very acidic tissue. This makes them much more susceptible to cancer, cardiovascular disease and premature aging.

If you have to drink tap water make sure it is filtered to eliminate chemicals especially chlorine which destroys friendly bacteria in your gut.

Q – CAN I SPICE UP MY WATER?

A – Go ahead and doctor up your water with shredded strawberries, oranges wedges, green tea or a touch of lemon.

Q – WHAT WILL HAPPEN IF I CHEAT DURING THE WEEK?

A – Well, first of all if you "cheat" during the week you will not stay in ketosis (fat burning). Now here is some good news- courtesy of "The Carbohydrate Addict's Diet. According to that diet plan you have to eat all your carbs within one hour. The idea is that if you only secrete insulin for one hour in a day then your body will not store any fat. We certainly do not recommend this if you are in Phase One of the Serial Killer Diet. Eating a high carb meal even within one hour will take your body out of ketosis.

Remember, our goal is for you to stay on this program. If you have to "cheat" midweek, then at least try and minimize your "cheating."

Q – WHAT ABOUT ALCOHOL?

A – Really, alcohol is not allowed during the week in Phase One or Phase Two. Alcohol converts to sugar pretty rapidly so we suggest waiting till Reward Days.

Q – WHAT ARE THE POSSIBLE SIDE EFFECTS OF THE SERIAL KILLER DIET?

A – 1) Nausea- If you are a carbo-holic your body might react to a drastic decrease in carbs. This may last for only the first week. Try not to get discouraged, this is very normal. Your body will take a few days to adjust.

– 2) Leg Cramps-When one drastically reduces carbs which supply electrolytes one should supplement with:

a) A good multi-vitamin mineral. Martin Clinic has a multi-vitamin called Martin Clinic Pro, 1-2 a day.

b) Potassium-approximately 200 mg. daily

c) Magnesium Citrate-400mg-1,000mg daily

– 3) Constipation-When you cut back on fruits and veggies you will reduce your fiber intake and therefore constipation is always possible. Drink lots of water and eat lots of nuts. Magnesium is helpful and adding a fiber supplement (Ultimate Fiber Plus) is always helpful.

– 4) Dehydration- It is essential on the Serial Killer Diet to drink a minimum of 2 liters a day or 64 ounces.

Q – WHEN SHOULD I EXPECT RESULTS?

A – Most people get results after a few days. They begin to feel more energy by the second week. Obviously everyone is different, but everyone who entered our study got results quickly and without exception.

Q – WHY START SUNDAY?

A – It will take 3 days to burn up carbohydrates as your primary source of fuel. So if you start on Sunday you will be burning fat by Wednesday.

Q – CAN I USE ARTIFICIAL SWEETENERS?

A – We at the Martin Clinic want you to understand that we try not to encourage the use of artificial sweeteners like aspartame, Splenda and others. We much prefer the use of Stevia. However, artificial sweeteners contain no carbs and could be used while the person is in Phase 1 of the Serial Killer Diet.

HIGH ENERGY AND FAT BURNING

This eating plan was formulated primarily to keep cortisol and insulin at normal levels. Anybody that has Chronic Fatigue or Fibromyalgia will benefit from following the Serial Killer Diet. When CFS patients cut back on carbs and replace it with healthy fat they experience a surge in energy and a loss of brain fog.

AVERAGE RESULTS

WEEK 1

♥2-3 inch fat loss around the belly

♥Increase in energy

♥Less bloating, less puffiness

WEEK 2

♥Another inch or two of fat loss

♥Energy levels increasing

♥More restful sleep

♥Noticed an improvement in skin tone

♥Improved appetite control-less cravings

♥Loss of brain fog

WEEK 3 and BEYOND

♥Continued fat loss

♥Improved blood sugar

♥Improved cholesterol levels

♥Reduced blood pressure

♥Some have even stopped snoring on this diet!

♥Less inflammation therefore less pain with those suffering from Fibromyalgia.

CHAPTER 9
SERIAL KILLER DIET RECIPES

By: Rose-Marie Martin, R.N.

CHAPTER 9

MY STORY

We at the Martin Clinic are doing research on 2 hormones that are playing havoc in society today. These Serial Killers are identified as the hormones cortisol – the stress hormone (excreted from the adrenal glands), and insulin (produced in the pancreas). When you secrete too much insulin due to poor eating habits (high carb diet) and cortisol due to stress, your body will feel lethargic and you will store fat. The Serial Killer Diet controls the production of these two hormones.

I personally, Rose-Marie Martin, could not believe how my supposedly "healthy" diet was so high in carbs. When I decided to try this way of eating I spent three afternoons in the grocery store reading labels. Then I started to read the label of the foods that I consistently buy each week. I have had a few "epiphany" moments in my life and this was definitely one of them! My MAJOR food group was carbohydrates and I didn't even realize it!

Over the years I had tried many "diets" and just became more frustrated as the scale would show weight loss but I still had the "sugar" belly. If you look around in a mall you will notice that women, more and more are developing the same shape especially in the stomach, waist area as men. Why is that?

The Serial Killer Diet is a fat-loss diet that works by forcing the body to burn fat by carbohydrate deprivation. This is a state where the body converts fat into ketones that the brain can use for fuel when glucose (carbohydrates) is in short supply. If you are doing it properly it takes about three days to start burning fat for fuel.

Most of the time, everyone in the world has their brain burning glucose. The brain can burn either glucose or ketones, but under normal circumstances ketones aren't produced by the body. The only time the body would create and burn ketones in large quantities are when there is not enough glucose available as a fuel source. The way to make glucose (a basic sugar) unavailable is to simply restrict carbohydrate consumption to 30g/day or less.

For example, if you stop eating all carbs on Sunday, this will deplete your liver and bloodstream of glucose, and your muscles of glycogen. At that point, your liver will start producing ketones, so the brain has a fuel to work with, and if you consume no carbohydrates at all, the body will start converting protein into glucose as it will still need at least 30g glucose per day. This is the start of your fat loss.

The first week I was not hungry and did not go through the brain fog that I normally suffered through at 11 am and 2 pm each day. In hindsight I realize that hunger is a signal that the body requires protein and fat and those who consume fruit and other foods without protein and fat (like me) will continue to be hungry and snack often throughout the day. Those who eat starches, (cereals, breads, potatoes, pastas and rice) when their bodies call for protein, will be hungry.

I also lost 2 full inches when I measured around my belly button. This alone was incentive to continue. The second week and those following I felt really good and energy level was higher than I ever used to have.

I have been on this diet for 5 months and I have not felt this good in several years. When I was diagnosed with Chronic Fatigue Syndrome and Fibromyalgia my husband started his research on how to get me better. Let's put it this way-I AM THE GUINEA PIG at the Martin Clinic. I can honestly say that my brain has never functioned at this level consistently for several years. My energy levels have improved dramatically and people around me have really noticed a big change. Besides feeling good, I've LOST 8 INCHES around my waist and 4 INCHES around each arm!!! This is why I highly recommend the Serial Killer diet-I am living proof!!

There are many benefits of the Serial Killer Diet, among them are:

1) Your body burns fat as its primary fuel source 24 hours a day, 5 ½ days a week. Thus, you will burn off adipose body fat at a rate no low carb-based diet can match. The other day and a half is your cheat time. It is very important to take this reward time.

2) People very often eat much less than when they're on carbs. For most people being on the Serial Killer Diet strongly blunts

hunger feelings, which makes it much easier to restrict calories.

3) This high fat, low carb diet also naturally spares lean muscle mass, far more than normal diets. Sparing lean muscle mass is incredibly important to dieters, as it helps to keep your metabolism from slowing down, which helps both in keeping the fat loss going, and with maintaining the fat loss.

4) The first fat to go is the "Belly Fat" or a better word for this is "Carb Belly". So remember to measure your waist around your belly button the first morning as you start this program.

The Serial Killer Diet allows for some unusual food choices, such as bacon, hamburgers, steak, ham, eggs, sausages, olives, and full-fat cheese. Now, most people have a hard time believing this when they have been told to avoid these foods and eat low fat or "light" because these foods are high in cholesterol, and high in saturated fats.

During the Serial Killer Diet, your body's primary fuel source is always 100% FAT (or ketones made from fat). For most people, the cholesterol never gets a chance to do damage, as not only is all the fat you eat converted to energy or ketones if you're doing things right, but also stored body fat is being burned at the same time!

SOME OF THE FOODS YOU SHOULD EAT

MEATS

Meats are a significant source of fat in our diets. Red meat is an excellent source of protein and energy. It was widely believed at one time that people who wanted to lose weight should not consume red meat due to its high fat content.

However, new studies have shown the opposite is true. It is now believed that consuming red meat can help in weight loss because it is more nutrient dense and satisfying than carb food consumption. Red meat can provide your body with essential nutrients like iron, zinc, Vitamin B12, Vitamin B6 and niacin. Moreover, it is found that the zinc in meat is absorbed better than zinc in grains and legumes.

VEGETABLES AND FRUIT

You might think that fruits and vegetables have no fat, but there are a couple of exceptions. Fat from fruit is good for you. An entire Florida avocado has 31 g of fat and net carbs of 9 grams. Avocados contain glutathione, one of the most potent antioxidants and disease-fighting agents available. Avocados are also a source of healthy fats and antioxidants that are good for any complexion.

Avocados can help to slow the release of sugars into the blood stream, thereby triggering less insulin release. Insulin, as previously stated, is the hormone that instructs the body to store energy as fat while preventing the use of stored energy.

If you enjoy green olives 6 of them contains 1.8 grams of fat and 0.1 net carbs.

SEAFOOD

Those who enjoy seafood will thoroughly enjoy the Serial Killer Diet since seafood contains fat the body needs, it's a good choice to fulfill daily fat requirements from seafood sources. Three ounces of mackerel contains 11.0 grams of fat and 0.0 net carbs while the same amount of herring provides 7.6 grams of fat and 0.0 net carbs. Three ounces of salmon contains 2.5 grams of fat and 0.0 net carbs. A 3.75-oz. can of sardines packed in oil contain 13 grams of fat and 0.0 net carbs.

DAIRY (NOT MILK)

Dairy products can contain a lot of fat, especially butter – 2 tsp. has 8 grams of fat and 0.0 net carbs. Just 2 tbsp. of cream cheese has 9 g of fat and 2.0 net carbs. One Mini BabyBel cheese provides 5 grams of fat and 0.0 net carbs. Meanwhile,

35% whipping cream contains 5 grams of fat and 0.0 net carbs. Just whip this up without sugar and put it on the low calorie jello to make a tasty dessert-and all for 0.0 net carbs.

NUTS AND SEEDS

Though nuts are high in fat, they are also nutritious. An ounce--28 g (10-12 kernels) of dry-roasted macadamia nuts has 21 g of fat and only 1.6 grams of carbs.. One ounce of pecans (19 halves) holds a whopping 20 grams of fat for only a net carb of 1.4 grams and almonds consists of 13.7 grams of fat and a total net carb of 2.7 and a sunflower seed for one ounce/28 grams holds 13.7 grams of fat for a net carb of 3.7 grams.

LOW CARB HEMP HEARTS

Here at Martin Clinic we love Hemp Hearts which are the most concentrated form of essentials with Omega Fats – 3, 6, 9 required for optimum human health. They can be sprinkled on your salad or put into a smoothie that Dr. Martin has developed. It is perfect along with Ultimate Fiber Plus for those troubled with constipation and for those avoiding carbohydrates.

THE SERIAL KILLER RECIPES

I have for the last several months compiled the following recipes that I know you will love. Most diets give you very little variation and you get bored eating the same foods NOT on the Serial Killer diet!!! It has been fun and a challenge to come up with recipes on how to de-carb my favourite foods and meals. I've often served people a low carb meal and low carb dessert without them even knowing that these foods were a part of the Serial Killer Diet. I even made my grandchildren the low carb cheesecake recipe and they LOVED it!

If you any menu ideas when you get started on the Serial Killer diet please share them with us at *info@martinclinic.com.*

SERIAL KILLER RECIPES

WHAT IS THE DIFFERENCE BETWEEN NET CARBS AND CARBS?

This confused me when I first started the diet. Carbs and Net Carbs are two different things. So the following is the explanation of how to calculate net carbs. It is very important to know your net carb total at the end of each day.

> This label says each 1 cup serving contains 31 grams of total carbohydrates and 0 gram of dietary fiber so the Net Carbs is 31 grams

Read the label and write down the total number of carbohydrates in one serving of the food you are trying to calculate the "net" carbs for.

(1) Start Here

(2) Check Calories

(3) Limit these Nutrients

(4) Get Enough of these Nutrients

(5) Footnote

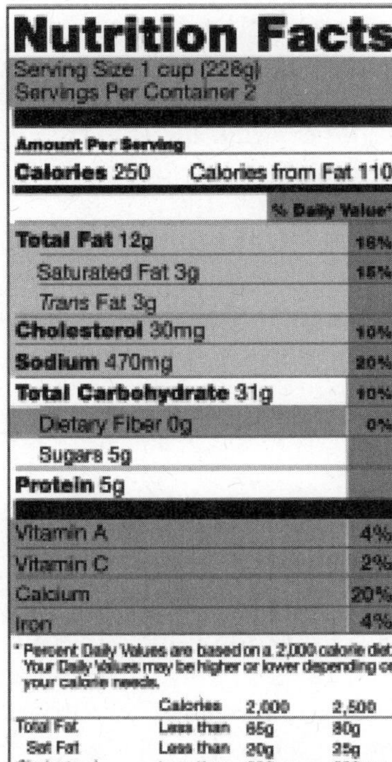

Nutrition Facts

Serving Size 1 cup (228g)
Servings Per Container 2

Amount Per Serving

Calories 250 Calories from Fat 110

	% Daily Value*
Total Fat 12g	18%
Saturated Fat 3g	15%
Trans Fat 3g	
Cholesterol 30mg	10%
Sodium 470mg	20%
Total Carbohydrate 31g	10%
Dietary Fiber 0g	0%
Sugars 5g	
Protein 5g	
Vitamin A	4%
Vitamin C	2%
Calcium	20%
Iron	4%

* Percent Daily Values are based on a 2,000 calorie diet. Your Daily Values may be higher or lower depending on your calorie needs.

	Calories	2,000	2,500
Total Fat	Less than	65g	80g
Sat Fat	Less than	20g	25g
Cholesterol	Less than	300mg	300mg
Sodium	Less than	2,400mg	2,400mg
Total Carbohydrate		300g	375g
Dietary Fiber		25g	30g

Write down the total fiber grams in the same serving.

Subtract the total fiber grams from the total carbohydrate grams. This will give you the "net" carb count for the food.

BALANCE YOUR ACID-ALKALINE CHEMISTRY

WHY?

A high acid overload can trigger symptoms like fatigue, headaches, digestive upset and weight gain. Acid overload creates internal inflammation that can harm vital organs. To prevent this damage the body shuttles acidic compounds into fat cells for storage. This gets the toxins out of circulation but it makes for unwanted weight gain. The more acid waste there is to store, the more fat the body will pack on. Drink lots of water to help eliminate acid waste.

A quick fix for acid overload is a diet rich in alkalinizing foods. Leafy greens like spinach, avocados, bell peppers, cucumbers, Swiss chard, parsley, celery, cabbage, lettuce, onion, cauliflower, broccoli and garlic. Some nuts, seeds and oils are also good sources of alkalinity; particularly almonds, flaxseeds, pumpkin seeds, coconut oil, fish oil, and cold pressed extra virgin olive oils. These foods are packed with bicarbonate, potassium and calcium-chemical buffers that work to neutralize acid in the body.

Most of the foods that contain alkaline minerals are the foods that we encourage you to eat on the low carb, high fat diet.

Sweets, alcohol, trans fats, pizza, colas, biscuits, chips, white bread, pasta, refined and processed foods should be avoided. Sugar should not be allowed as it feeds the yeast in your body which thrives in an acidic environment.

When you reduce acid waste your body no longer has need to hold on to excess fat!!

ALMOND FLOUR/MEAL ***GLUTEN FREE - THE MARTIN CLINIC DISCOVERY!!*

For 1 cup of Almond flour/meal has - fat (the good fat) – 56grams; fiber = 48 grams, carbs =24 grams. Remember how to get the difference from carbs to net carbs? Subtract the total fiber grams (48 grams) from the total carbohydrate grams (24 grams). This will give you the “net” carb count for the food. For almond flour/meal the **NET CARB IS -24 GRAMS-THAT’S RIGHT MINUS 24 GRAMS!!**

Almond flour, sometimes called almond meal, is made from raw blanched almonds. The almonds are ground into a powder that you can use instead of wheat flour in cookies, cakes and other foods. It is sometimes used by people who are allergic to wheat gluten. Although almond flour is similar in consistency to wheat flour, its nutritional makeup is significantly different.

Almond flour packs 56 g of fat into each serving. Although almond flour has a higher total fat content, the fat is made up of fatty acids that were shown to reduce cholesterol levels in a 2002 study conducted by Canadian researchers. The fat in almond flour comes mainly from monounsaturated and polyunsaturated fats. There is 24g of protein and the fiber content is 48g. This gives 1 cup (112g) -24g of net carbs. You read it right-minus 24g net carbs/serving.

Amid a widespread awareness of gluten-free diets, almond flour is a common substitute for traditional wheat flour. The sweet, nutty flavour from almond flour can be added to nearly any recipe that calls for flour, including cakes, cookies, desserts and main dishes.

HOMEMADE ALMOND MEAL/FLOUR

INGREDIENTS AND PREPARATION:

An alternative to purchasing almond flour is to prepare it yourself using a food processor.

Simply place 1/4 cup of almonds (into a Vita-Mix or a good blender) and grind for several seconds.

Sift the ground almonds.

Store the almond flour in the refrigerator because almond flour deteriorates more quickly than wheat flour.

You get about 35 percent of your vitamin E requirement for the day, 20 percent of your magnesium needs and 6 percent of your daily requirement for both iron and calcium. Your body uses vitamin E for the health of your red blood cells, and magnesium for your muscle function, bone strength and energy needs.

Add almond flour to baked goods. You can substitute the wheat flour with almond flour in recipes for cakes, cookies and muffins. The almond flour provides a moist, coarse texture.

ALMOND FLOUR USES:

1) You can coat meats and vegetables for a breading substitute. You can use the almond flour on beef, fish or chicken similar to cracker crumbs or wheat flour.

2) Replace up to 1/4 cup of almond flour per cup of wheat flour. Almond flour doesn't contain gluten that causes baked goods to rise, but this ratio allows the goods to rise.

3) Create your own dishes. You can easily form your own recipes using ingredients such as almond flour, eggs, vanilla and spices. **For example, add 1 cup of almond meal, three eggs and 1/8 tsp. of pure vanilla extract for <u>gluten-free pancakes.</u>**

*Store the almond flour in the refrigerator or freezer. This prevents the almond flour from going stale.

Almond flour is good in "quick-bread" type recipes, like muffins, nut breads, and pancakes.

SOME EXAMPLES OF NET CARB IN FOODS

FOOD	SERVING	CARBS	FIBER	NET CARBS
Fruit				
Apple (fruit)	5 oz.	21.1 g	3 g	18.1 g
Apricots (fruit)	3 (4 oz. ea.)	11.8 g	3 g	8.8 g
Avocado (fruit)	1/2 (3 oz.)	7.4 g	2.5 g	4.9 g
Blackberries (fruit)	1 cup	18.4 g	7.2 g	11.2 g
Bluebrries (fruit)	1 cup	20.5 g	3.3 g	17.2 g
Cantaloupe (fruit)	1 cup	13.4 g	1.3 g	12.1 g
Cranberries (fruit)	1/2 cup	6 g	2 g	4 g
Grapefruit (fruit)	1/2 (4 oz)	9.5 g	0.7 g	8.8 g
Grapes (fruit)	1 cup	15.5 g	0.6 g	14.9 g
Guava (fruit)	1 (about 3 oz)	10.7 g	4.9 g	5.8 g
Kiwi (fruit)	1 (2 1/2 oz)	11 g	2.6 g	8.4 g
Mango (fuit)	1/2 (3 1/2 oz)	17.6 g	2.1 g	15.5 g
Nectarine (fruit)	1 (5 oz)	16 g	2.2 g	13.8 g
Orange (Fruit)	1 (4 1/2 oz)	15.4 g	3.1 g	12.3 g
Papaya (fruit)	1/2 (5 1/2 oz)	14.9 g	2.6 g	12.3 g
Peach (fruit)	1	9.7 g	1/4 g	8.3
Pear (fruit)	1 (6 oz)	25.1 g	4.3 g	20.8 g
Pineapple (fruit)	1 cup	19.2 g	1.9 g	8.2 g

FOOD	SERVING	CARBS	FIBER	NET CARBS
Rasberries (fruit)	1 cup	14.2 g	6 g	8.2 g
Strawberries (fruit)	1 cup	10.5 g	3.9 g	6.6 g
Tangarine (fruit)	1 (3 oz)	9.4 g	N/A	9.4 g
Watermelon (fruit)	1 cup	11.5 g	0.6 g	10.9 g
Nuts				
Almonds	1 oz	5.8 g	1.9 g	3.9 g
Brazil Nuts	1 oz	3.6 g	1.6 g	2 g
Cashews	1 oz	9.3 g	0.9 g	8.4 g
Coconut, raw	1 oz	4.3 g	2.5 g	1.8 g
Peanuts	1 oz	6 g	2.2 g	1.8 g
Pecans	1 oz	5.2 g	1.9 g	3.3 g
Pistachios	1 oz	7.1 g	3.1 g	4 g
Pumpkin Seeds	1 oz hulled	5.1 g	3.9 g	1.2 g
Sesame Seeds	1 Tbsp.	0.8 g	0.8 g	0 g
Sunflower	1 oz	5.3 g	1.9 g	3.4 g
Walnuts	1 oz	3.4 g	1.4 g	2 g
Cheese				
American Cheese	1 oz	0.5 g	N/A	0.5 g
Blue Cheese	1 oz	0.7 g	N/A	0.7 g
Chedder (cheese)	1 oz	3 g	N/A	3 g

FOOD	SERVING	CARBS	FIBER	NET CARBS
Cottage (cheese)	1/2 cup	3 g	N/A	3 g
Cream Cheese	1 oz	0.7 g	N/A	0.7 g
Feta Cheese	1 oz	1.2 g	N/A	1.2 g
Jack Cheese	1 oz	0.2 g	N/A	0.2 g
Mozzarella Cheese	1 oz	0.8 g	N/A	0.8 g
Parmesan Cheese	1 Tbsp	0.2 g	N/A	0.2 g
Provolone Cheese	1 oz	0.6 g	N/A	0.6 g
Ricotta Cheese	1/2 cup	6.4 g	N/A	6.4 g
Swiss Cheese	1 oz	1 g	N/A	1 g

Vegetables

FOOD	SERVING	CARBS	FIBER	NET CARBS
Alfalfa Sprouts (veg)	1/2 cup raw	0.6 g	N/A	0.6 g
Asparagus (veg)	1/2 cup boiled	4 g	1.5 g	2.5 g
Broccoli (veg)	1/2 cup boiled	4 g	2 g	2 g
Brussels Sprouts (veg)	1/2 cup boiled	6.8 g	3.4 g	3.4 g
Chinese Cabbage (veg)	1/2 cup boiled	1.5 g	1.4 g	0.1 g
Common Cabbage (veg)	1/2 cup boiled	3.5 g	1.8 g	1.7 g
Red Cabbage (veg)	1/2 cup boiled	3.5 g	1.8 g	1.7 g
Carrot (veg)	1 (2 1/2 oz)	7.3 g	2.3 g	5 g

FOOD	SERVING	CARBS	FIBER	NET CARBS
	3 florets	2.8 g	1.3 g	1.5 g
Celery (veg)	1/2 cup diced	2.2 g	1 g	1.2 g
Sweet Corn (veg)	1 ear	19.3 g	2.9 g	16.4 g
Cucumber (veg)	5 oz raw	4.4 g	1.5 g	2.9 g
Eggplant (veg)	1/2 cup boiled	3.2 g	1.2 g	2 g
Garlic (veg)	1 clove	1 g	trace	1 g
	1 Tbsp raw	0.9 g	0.1 g	0.8 g
Lettuce				
Butter head (veg)	1 cup raw	1 g	0.4 g	0.6 g
Iceberg (veg)	1 cup raw	2.8 g	1.4 g	1.12 g
Romaine (veg)	1 cup raw	1.3 g	1 g	0.3 g
Mushrooms (veg)	1/2 cup boiled	4 g	1.7 g	2.3 g
Okra (veg)	1/2 cup boiled	5.8 g	2.6 g	3.2 g
Onions (veg)	1/2 cup boiled	6.9 g	1.3 g	5.6 g
Chili Peppers (veg)	1 Tbsp. raw	0.9 g	0.1 g	0.8 g
Green Bell Peppers (veg)	1/2 cup raw	3.2 g	0.8 g	2.4 g
Red Bell Peppers (veg)	1/2 cup raw	3.2 g	0.8 g	2.4 g
Radishes (veg)	1/2 cup raw	2 g	1.3 g	0.7 g
Scallions (veg)	1/2 cup boiled	3.7 g	1.2 g	2.5 g

FOOD	SERVING	CARBS	FIBER	NET CARBS
Spinach (veg)	1/2 cup boiled	3.4 g	2 g	1.4 g
Swiss Chard (veg)	1/2 cup boiled	3.6 g	1.8 g	1.8 g

METRIC CONVERSION TABLE FOR BAKING

1 ml = 1/5 teaspoon

5 ml = 1 teaspoon

15ml = 1 tablespoon

30 ml = 1 fluid ounce or 28 grams

100 ml = 3.4 fluid ounce

240 ml = 1 cup

1 liter = 34 fluid ounce, or 4.2 cups, 2.1 pints

1 gram = 0.35 ounce

28 grams = 1 ounce

100 grams = 3.5 ounces

454 grams = 1 pound, 16 ounces, (1 cup)

500 grams = 1.10 pounds

1 kilogram = 2.2 pounds, or 35 ounces

1 cup = 16 ounces, or 16 tablespoons

THESE CONDIMENTS HAVE 0 CARBS

Mustard (except sweetened mustards, especially honey mustard)

Cider and wine vinegars

Most bottled hot sauces (such as Tabasco)

Most salsas

Soy sauce

Mayonnaise

Sugar-free salad dressings, preferably brands high in monounsaturated fat, such as olive oil (check labels carefully)

Capers

Horseradish

Pesto

Herbs and spices (but watch for mixtures with added sugars)

Lemon or lime juice (1 gram of carb per tablespoon)

Extracts, (vanilla, lemon, almond, etc.)

Broth or bouillon

VARIABLE CARBS – CHECK LABELS

Balsamic vinegar

Rice wine vinegar

Worcestershire sauce

Included in all low carb diets, most meat contains zero carbs. Only crumbed, battered or breaded meat contains carbohydrate, which is added during processing. Most meats are a useful source of nutrients, like protein, minerals and vitamins.

MEAT	AMOUNT	CARBS	FIBER	NET CARB
Chicken	4 oz	0 g	0 g	0 g
Turkey	4 oz	0 g	0 g	0 g
Beef Steak	6 oz	0 g	0 g	0 g
Roast Beef	6 oz	0 g	0 g	0 g
Ham	4 oz	0 g	0 g	0 g
Hot Dog	1	2 g	0 g	2 g
Pork Chop	6 oz	0 g	0 g	0 g
Breakfast Sausage	1 link	2 g	0 g	2 g
Pork Sausage	1 link	4 g	0 g	4 g
Salami	1 link	1 g	0 g	1 g
Balogna	2 slices	2 g	0 g	2 g
Pepperoni	1 oz	0.5 g	0 g	0.5 g

MAGNIFICENT WAYS TO JAZZ UP YOUR 0 CARB CONDIMENTS

MUSTARD

½ cup mustard

2 tbsp. chopped fresh parsley

1 tsp. each of minced thyme and rosemary

Blend all ingredients together

Serve on grilled steak

PESTO

½ cup mayonnaise

Stir in 2 tbsp. prepared pesto

2 tbsp. chopped fresh parsley

Spread on grilled chicken

SALSA

1/2 cup salsa, mild medium or hot

Stir in 4 oz. cream cheese at room temperature until mixture is well combined.

Serve over low carb stir fried veggies.

SOUR CREAM

½ cup sour cream

Stir in 1 tbsp. chopped dill

1 minced garlic clove

½ cup chopped cucumbers and a squeeze of lemon.

Serve over fish

CAESAR MAYONNAISE

½ cup mayonnaise

Purée with 1 anchovy fillet

1 garlic clove

¼ cup parmesan cheese

½ lemon juiced

Blend together until smooth

Toss with romaine lettuce

VINAIGRETTE

½ cup of a mixture of extra virgin olive oil and vinegar

Stir in ½ tsp. cumin

2 tbsp. chopped fresh parsley

Sea salt and pepper to taste

½ chopped garlic clove

Drizzle over cucumber salad

DE-CARB YOUR FAVOURITES

I firmly believe that to make low-carb eating into a way of life (instead of a "diet"), it's IMPORTANT to find low-carb versions of a lot of your favourite meals.

BREAKFAST RECIPES

BREAKFAST

3 sausage links = 6 carbs

3 Schneider's bacon strips (because this brand has no carbs)

2 eggs any style = 0 carbs

Coffee black or with stevia or Splenda, 35% whipping cream= 0 carbs

Nutritional Information: 6 Net Carbs

OR

DR. MARTIN'S PERFECT SMOOTHIE FOR SERIAL KILLER DIET

4 Strawberries = 4 net carbs

4 ounces water

4 ounces 35% whipping cream

1-2 scoops Hemp Seed Protein or Whey Protein Isolate

2 tbsp. Coconut oil or 2 tbsps. Macadamia Nut Oil

1 tsp. ground cinnamon

1 tbsp. flaxseed

Nutritional Information: 4 Net Carbs

DID U KNOW?

CINNAMON

1) Studies have shown that just 1/2 teaspoon of cinnamon per day can lower LDL cholesterol.

2) Several studies suggest that cinnamon may have a regulatory effect on blood sugar, making it especially beneficial for people

with Type 2 diabetes.

3) In some studies, cinnamon has shown an amazing ability to stop medication-resistant yeast infections.

4) It has an anti-clotting effect on the blood.

5) When added to food, it inhibits bacterial growth and food spoilage, making it a natural food preservative.

6) It is a great source of manganese, fiber, iron, and calcium.

DID U KNOW?

FLAXSEEDS

Eating flaxseed is the best thing you can do for your health and your waistline. The seeds lignans cleanse the digestive tract of up to six pounds of waste per week, plus help enhance the liver's metabolism of body fat.

If you are not used to a lot of fiber, you may not want to start with a whole recipe of the following cereal recipe. It hss 10 grams of fiber, and one third of that is soluble, which is good for you, but it's a lot at once. That said, it's yummy, low-carb, quick to make, and will help see you through the morning!

LOW CARB CEREAL

INGREDIENTS:

1/4 cup grounded flax seed

1/2 cup boiling water

2 tbsp. crunchy peanut butter

1/4 tbsp. cinnamon

1 tsp. pure vanilla extract

¼ cup 35% heavy cream

2 tbsp. unsweetened maple flavoured syrup

Optional: ½ scoop of your favourite protein powder

*Note that a half recipe would be 2 Tbsp. flax meal, 1/4 cup water, and 1 Tbsp. peanut butter.

PREPARATION:

Pour boiling water over flax seed meal and stir well.

Stir in crunchy peanut butter and cinnamon.

Let thicken for 1 to 2 minutes.

Add unsweetened maple syrup

Pour 35% heavy cream over top

Stir well

Nutritional Information: Each recipe has 5 grams of net carbs; 10 grams of fiber, 14 grams protein, 29 grams of fat.

LOW CARB GRANOLA

Feel free to substitute any nuts or seeds you like in this recipe, but the ground flax is essential, and the coconut is helpful. These will absorb the liquids and this is what will form the clumps -- otherwise you just have toasted nuts and seeds with some flavouring.

INGREDIENTS:

1 cup raw almonds

1 cup raw walnuts

1 cup raw pecans

1 cup shredded coconut, unsweetened

1/2 cup sunflower seeds

1/2 cup flax seed meal

1/2 teaspoon salt

1/2 cup water

1/2 cup butter or coconut oil

1/2 cup sugar-free maple-flavoured syrup (E.D. Smith sweetened with sucralose or Stevia 2 grams-.75 ounces)

PREPARATION:

Pre-heat oven to 300 F.

Cover baking sheet with sides with a silicon mat or greased parchment paper.

Roughly chop the nuts.

*You can do this in a food processor, but if you do, start with the harder nuts -- the almonds in this recipe if you use them. Once they are chopped up a bit you can add the softer nuts (walnuts, pecans). Otherwise the softer ones will become ground too much before the hard ones are chopped.

Melt the butter or coconut oil - you can microwave it in the bowl you're going to use for mixing (although you can mix right on the baking sheet), if you wish.

Mix the syrup and coconut oil or butter together.

Combine the nuts, coconut, seeds, and salt. If you're doing this on the baking sheet, add the water first and mix (hands work best), and then the oil/butter and syrup mixture. Otherwise, just combine it all in a bowl and turn out onto the baking sheet. Press into an even layer.

**At this point, it's good to taste it. Judge your own desire for sweetness and add more if you want.

Bake for 30-40 minutes. Twice during the baking, stir the mixture with a large spoon and press back down. After the second time, don't move it around anymore. Bake until fragrant and lightly browned on the surface.

Let cool completely in pan. It will crisp as it cools.

Store in sealed container.

Make about 6 cups -- 12 servings.

Nutritional Information: Each serving has 4 g net carbs; 6 grams fiber; 7 grams protein.

QUICK MICROWAVE BLUEBERRY ALMOND BREAKFAST PUDDING

This easy, healthy, low carb breakfast pudding can be made with any berries or other additions as listed. Make it in the microwave in less than 5 minutes.

For a larger serving, increase the almond meal up to 1/2 cup, add 1 Tbsp. water, and cook a bit longer.

INGREDIENTS:

1/3 cup almond meal

2 Tablespoons water

1 egg

1/4 cup blueberries - frozen or otherwise

¼ tsp. almond extract

Sweetener and flavouring (cinnamon or pure vanilla extract to taste)

PREPARATION:

Mix almond meal, egg, and water in a microwave-safe bowl.

Dash of vanilla or cinnamon.

Microwave on high for about 45 seconds.

Move the cooked part of the pudding towards the center of the bowl and add blueberries and/or any mix-ins you want.

Microwave for about 45-60 more seconds, depending on mix-ins (**frozen** fruit will need even longer cooking, as it will cool down the pudding).

Stir and eat.

Possible Additions:

Fresh or frozen berries or other fruit (Low Carb Fruit List)

Unsweetened coconut

Peanut butter or other nut butters

Small cubes of cream cheese (low carb)

Sugar-free maple or other low carb syrup

Chopped nuts

*I make this all in a mug. Very much like a hot blueberry muffin eaten with a fork. I put everything in at once - I microwaved it for 1 ½ minute. Put a cover over your cup as the blueberries explode especially if they are frozen, but it tastes great. Yummy!

Nutritional Information: Each serving (with blueberries) has 6 g Net Carbs; 5 grams fiber, 13 grams protein.

CHEESY EGG PUFFS

INGREDIENTS:

½ cup fresh white mushrooms, sliced = 1.5 net carbs

½ cup chopped green onions = 2 net carbs

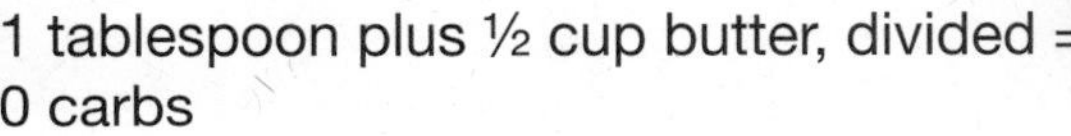

1 tablespoon plus ½ cup butter, divided = 0 carbs

½ cup low carb baking mix = 11 net carbs

1 teaspoon salt

10 eggs, lightly beaten = 3.0 net carbs, protein 53g

3 cups shredded Monterey Jack cheese =2.5 net carbs, protein 87.9

1 cup small curd cottage cheese 8.3 net carb, protein 24.9

Total = 28.3 for 2 dozen, approximately 1.1 net carbs/ egg puff

PREPARATION:

Sauté the mushrooms, and onions in 1 tablespoon butter until tender, in a frying pan.

Combine the flour, baking powder and salt in a large bowl and in another bowl

Mix in eggs and cheese. Melt remaining butter and add to egg mixture.

Stir into dry ingredients along with mushroom mixture.

Fill greased muffin cups three-fourths full.

Bake at 350° for 35-40 minutes.

Carefully run the knife around the edge of the muffin cups before removing.

BREAKFAST EGGS AND BACON

Line greased muffin tins with half-cooked bacon slices.

Slip an egg into center of each

Sprinkle each with salt and pepper to taste.

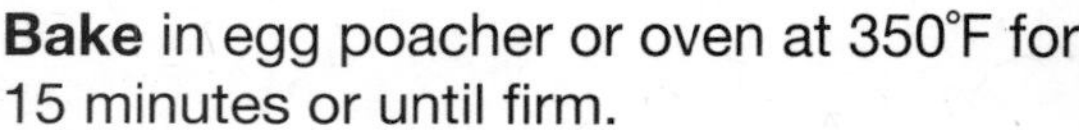

Bake in egg poacher or oven at 350°F for 15 minutes or until firm.

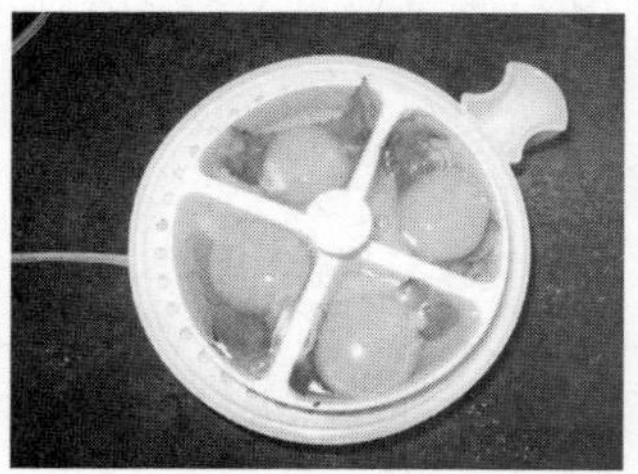

Nutritional Information: Depending on the net carb of the bacon that is used this recipe can be 0-2 net carbs.

DID U KNOW?

EGGS

1) Eggs make it easy to get slim because they provide the maximum protein power. Numerous studies –including a recent one at the University of Connecticut "have shown very clearly that protein at breakfast provides significant advantages in terms of weight control," notes the Egg Nutrition Center's Helenbeth Reynolds, R.D. "Yet for many of us, breakfast remains the lowest protein meal of the day." Eggs are a very easy way to transform your morning. "They're packed with protein, vitamins, minerals and antioxidants. One more benefit: They're linked to improved energy levels!

2) They shut down hunger. Though all protein helps shut down

hunger hormones, eggs happen to boast the highest quality protein. "Eggs are the gold standard'" beating even milk or meat, notes University of Kansan egg researcher Heather J. Leidy, PhD. So eggs not only kill hunger but are much better than bagels or cereal and beat other forms of protein.

3) They reduce fat storage and boost metabolism! Eggs provide more amino acids than other protein sources. This factor helps them protect our high metabolism muscle tissue as we lose weight. Even more importantly choosing eggs instead of carbohydrate rich foods means our bodies make less of the fat storage hormone-insulin. A Louisiana State University study found that eating eggs for breakfast helped dieters lose 65% more weight.

PANCAKES

1 cup low carb mix or 1cup almond meal

1 tsp. coconut oil (melted)

2 eggs

½ tsp. baking powder

½ tsp. vanilla extract

¾ cup 35% cream

PREPARATION:

Blend all ingredients together in listed order and cook in pan with a bit of oil as you would any pancakes.

Nutritional Information: Net Carbs= 6g.

DID U KNOW?

HEALTHY OMEGA 3 OILS

All fats are not created equal! Extra Virgin Olive oil delivers a "stop eating signal"! When a healthy fat like olive, coconut or flax seed oil hits the intestinal wall (just 1 tsp.), it releases CCK (cholecystokinin) a hormone that sends a "stop eating" message to the brain. If using olive oil, it is best to use the Extra Virgin Olive Oil because it is the least processed olive oil, so it has the most antioxidants and provides the greatest health benefits.

LOW CARB MUFFINS

INGREDIENTS:

2 cups almond flour/almond meal

2 teaspoons baking powder

1/4 teaspoon salt

1/2 cup (1 stick) butter, melted

4 eggs

1/3 cup water

1/3 cup sweetener of choice

PREPARATION:

Preheat oven to 350 F.

Butter a muffin tin. You can really do it with any size, but I'm basing the recipe on a 12-muffin tin.

Mix dry ingredients together well.

Add wet ingredients and mix thoroughly (You don't want strings of egg white in there and you don't have to worry about "tunnels" when you are using almond meal).

Put batter in muffin tins (about 1/2 to 2/3 full) and bake for about 15 minutes.

Variations: Add 1 cup fresh or frozen blueberries or strawberries.

Nutritional Information: Each muffin has 2g net carbs plus 2 grams fiber, 6 g protein.

LUNCH RECIPES

LUNCH-SALAD

4 cups chopped romaine or other dark green lettuce (not iceberg),

Half an avocado

4 ounces cooked chicken meat, with your favourite low carb dressing.

DID U KNOW?

AVOCADO

1) Oleic acid in avocado can be used to lower cholesterol level in the blood.

2) Avocado includes necessary minerals like potassium, calcium, vitamin C and K, folic acid, copper, sodium and dietary fibres. These are used to provide the mineral necessities of the body.

3) Potassium in avocado helps regulate blood pressure.

4) It improves the ability of the body to absorb carotenoids.

5) It is a good antioxidant.

6) Avocado can be used in the treatment of skin disorders.

7) It is used to heal people who suffer from digestive and circulatory problems.

The avocado can be a helpful part of a successful weight-management program. It brings several advantages:

– Its monounsaturated fat speeds up the basal metabolic rate, as compared with saturated fat.

– Its high good fat content provides a quicker feeling of satiation ("fullness"), thus helping to reduce overeating.

– Its high fat content reduces the temptation to binge on foods high in sugars or saturated fats.

– It is rich in vitamins and minerals.

TURKEY SALAD

INGREDIENTS:

3 cups shredded romaine lettuce

1 cup torn watercress leaves or arugula

1 sliced medium cucumber

1 sweet red pepper, thinly sliced

2 cups cubed cooked turkey

1 avocado peeled, pitted and cubed

¼ cup blue or feta cheese, crumbled

2 hard-cooked eggs, sliced

2 tsp. chopped chives or green onions

PREPARATION:

Arrange romaine on a large platter, top with watercress or arugula.

Place cucumber, red pepper, turkey, avocado, cheese and eggs on top.

Sprinkle with chives.

Pour dressing over and toss.

DRESSING:

2 Tbsp. red wine vinegar

½ tsp. Dijon mustard

1 clove minced garlic

Salt and pepper to taste

3 tbsp. of extra virgin olive oil

PREPARATION:

Stir together in a small bowl, vinegar, mustard, garlic, salt and pepper.

Whisk the oil in gradually.

Nutritional Information: 9g carbs, 5g of fiber, 4g net carbs.

SWEET AND SOUR LIME DRESSING

INGREDIENTS:

1 tsp. lime juice (from a bottle is fine)

1 tsp. water

2 tsp. extra virgin olive oil

Seasonings to taste

Sweetener (Stevia or Sucralose) to taste

PREPARATION:

Pour lime juice and water in bowl. Add sweetener to the tanginess level you want.

Add sea salt and pepper.

Whisk in the olive oil.

Nutritional Information: 0 Net Carb

LOW CARB BROCCOLI AND BACON SALAD

INGREDIENTS:

1 large stalk of broccoli (chopped to about 2.5 cups of florets and peeled stem)

1/4 lb. bacon (cooked until crisp and chopped)

1/4 cup finely chopped onion

1/2 cup mayonnaise

1 and 1/2 tablespoons lemon juice, (or to taste)

1/4 cup sunflower seeds

Salt and pepper (to taste)

PREPARATION:

Blanch broccoli by either boiling it or microwaving it for 1 to 2 minutes. It should still be crunchy, just not as hard as when it's raw. Quickly cool it by running it under cold tap water.

To make your dressing, mix mayonnaise, lemon juice, sweetener, and a pinch each of salt and pepper (adjust to taste). Add onions.

Mix the broccoli, dressing and remaining ingredients together. Save a little of the sunflower seeds and bacon to sprinkle over the top.

Nutritional Information: Net Carbs= 3g.

Optional: ½ cup of shredded cheese sprinkled on top

DID YOU KNOW?

CARBOHYDRATE AND FIBER COUNTS FOR CAULIFLOWER

– ½ cup cauliflower (50 grams): 1.5 grams net carbs plus 1 gram fiber and 12 calories

– 1 medium head of cauliflower (5-6" diameter; about 20 oz): 16 grams net carbs plus 14 grams fiber and 144 calories

– ¼ lb. (4 oz.) cauliflower: 3 grams net carbs plus 3 gram fiber and 28 calories

"POTATO", CAULIFLOWER SALAD

INGREDIENTS:

1 medium head cauliflower (about 4 cups/1 quart florets)

2 hard-boiled eggs

1 medium stalk celery, minced (including leaves)

½ cup chopped green pepper

2 onions, chopped

1/3 cup mayonnaise

1 tablespoon prepared mustard

1 teaspoon lemon juice

¼ teaspoon garlic powder

¼ teaspoon onion powder

Pinch of cayenne pepper (optional)

1-2 teaspoons sugar substitute

2 tablespoons sugar-free pickle relish or dill relish, or chopped sugar-free pickle

Salt and pepper

Your own preference of seasoning-to taste

PREPARATION:

Break or chop the cauliflower into small florets.

Microwave florets in a covered container with a small amount of water, or steam on the stove.

Drain and put into a medium bowl.

Place into fridge to cool.

Chop the egg and add.

Toss with salt and pepper.

Mix the ingredients for the dressing (mayo, lemon juice, spices, etc.). Taste for the balance of flavours you like. Mix the chopped vegetables and the dressing into the cauliflower and egg mixture.

Add chopped fresh herbs if you wish - chives, dill, or parsley work well,

Chill.

Makes 8 servings

Nutritional Information: Each serving has 3 grams net carbs plus 1.5 grams fiber, 3 grams protein, and 99 calories.

SPINACH SALAD WITH WARM BACON DRESSING

INGREDIENTS:

1 package baby spinach (about 9-10 oz) or that much washed spinach leaves

4 pieces of thick-cut bacon or 6 pieces thin cut (about 150

grams), chopped

1 hard-boiled egg, sliced

¼ cup minced onion

1 clove garlic

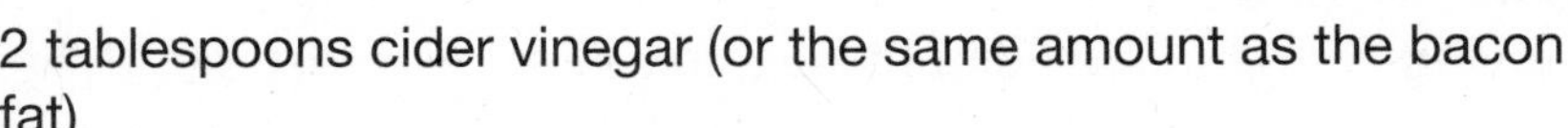

2 tablespoons cider vinegar (or the same amount as the bacon fat)

A pinch of salt

Two pinches of pepper

2 teaspoons sugar substitute

PREPARATION:

Put the spinach (and other vegetables if you like) in a large bowl. The spinach will shrink down some in the hot dressing, but you need room to work.

Chop the bacon and fry until crisp. Remove with slotted spoon and drain on paper towels.

If you like a lightly dressed salad, leave about 2 Tablespoons of the bacon fat in the pan. If you want more dressing, leave more fat and then balance it with more vinegar and a bit more sweetener. (This dressing is a sweet and sour sort of thing.)

Cook the onion in the fat for 2-3 minutes, and then add the garlic - cook for 15-30 seconds or until it is starting to be fragrant. Be careful not to brown the garlic or it will get bitter.

Add the vinegar, and scrape up the brown bits in the pan. (The vinegar will seem potent, but it mellows quickly with the heat and sweetener.) Add the salt, pepper, and sweetener. Stir to dissolve, and pour the dressing over the spinach.

Toss the spinach until coated. Transfer to individual plates or bowls and top with bacon bits and other toppings as desired.

Slice and divide the egg over top of the salad.

This makes three large servings as a side dish.

Nutritional Information: Each serving has 3.5 grams net carbs plus 2.5 grams fiber, 9 grams protein,

This warm Spinach salad can easily be made into a meal by adding chopped cooked chicken, turkey, or even fish or tofu. Chopped egg is also a classic option. If you want more vegetables, mushrooms and red pepper work especially well.

DID U KNOW?

HEALTH BENEFITS OF SPINACH

It is difficult to overestimate the nutritional powerhouse of spinach. Here are some reasons why spinach is so beneficial.

1) Diet - One cup of spinach has nearly 20% of the RDA of dietary fiber, which aids in digestion, prevents constipation, maintains low blood sugar, and curbs overeating.

2) Flavonoids - phytonutrients with anti-cancer properties abundant in spinach -- have been shown to slow down cell division in human stomach and skin cancer cells. Furthermore, spinach has shown that it provides significant protection against the occurrence of aggressive prostate cancer.

3) Anti-Inflammatory - Spinach contains compounds that play an important role in the regulation of inflammation and are present in unusually high amounts.

4) Antioxidants - Vitamin C, vitamin E, beta-carotene, manganese, zinc and selenium, present in spinach, all serve as powerful antioxidants that combat the onset of osteoporosis, atherosclerosis and high blood pressure. Both antioxidants lutein and zeaxanthin are especially plentiful in spinach and protect the eye from cataracts and age-related macular degeneration.

5) Blood Pressure - By inhibiting the angiotensin I-converting enzyme, peptides within spinach have been shown to effectively

lower blood pressure.

6) Immunity - One cup of spinach contains over 337% of the RDA of vitamin A that not only protects and strengthens "entry points" into the human body, such as mucous membranes, respiratory, urinary and intestinal tracts, but is also a key component of lymphocytes (or white blood cells) that fight infection.

7) Skin - The high amount of vitamin A in spinach also promotes healthy skin by allowing for proper moisture retention in the epidermis, thus fighting psoriasis, keratinization, acne and even wrinkles.

8) Bones - One cup of boiled spinach provides over 1000% of the RDA of vitamin K that can prevent excess activation of the cells that break down bones, as well as promotes the protein that is essential for maintaining the strength and density of our bones.

9) Brain and Nervous System Function - The abundance of vitamin K in spinach contributes greatly to a healthy nervous system and brain function by providing an essential nutrient that assists in the making of the crucial fat that makes up the Myelin sheath around our nerves.

BLAST BELLY FAT WITH OUR SLIMMING SALAD

INGREDIENTS:

Arrange 6 cups of spinach on a serving platter.

Top with 10 sliced mushrooms

Slice 4 medium strawberries and scatter on top

2 tbsp. pine nuts or slivered almonds

½ cup chopped cucumbers

2 tbsp. basil

PREPARATION:

In a bowl whisk ¼ cup each of extra virgin olive oil and fresh lime juice.

Add 1 tsp. ground cinnamon

¾ tsp. salt and 1/8 tsp. pepper

Drizzle over salad

Toss and serve

Serves 6

Nutritional Information: Per Serving Net Carbs = 1.3 g

BLUE CHEESE SALAD DRESSING – ALWAYS LOOK FOR THE BRAND THAT HAS 0-1 CARB/ TABLESPOON

INGREDIENTS:

1 cup regular mayonnaise

1 cup sour cream

6 oz. blue cheese

1 tbsp. apple cider or wine vinegar

1/ 2 teaspoon pepper

2 teaspoons Worcestershire sauce (optional)

1/2 teaspoon garlic powder (optional)

PREPARATION:

Crumble the blue cheese, and mix all ingredients together.

Thin with water if desired.

Nutritional Information: 2 tablespoons of dressing has less than one gram of carbohydrate, and about 2 grams of protein

CABBAGE SOUP

INGREDIENTS:

2 cups cooked ground beef

2/3 cup shredded cabbage

1/2 of a 430 ml. jar mild, medium or hot salsa

3 tbsp. 35% heavy cream

1 cup water

½ cup tomato juice

2 tbsp. chopped onion

Salt and pepper to taste

PREPARATION:

Fry ground beef in a frying pan

Transfer to soup pot

Add 2/3 cups of shredded cabbage

Mix in salsa and 3 tbsp. of cream

Combine water and ½ cup tomato juice with the chopped onions and add to pot

Stir altogether

Season to taste

Simmer in pot for 20 minutes

Serves 3-4

Nutritional Information: Shredded cabbage= 3.4 net carbs; Salsa = 3 net carbs; ½ cup tomato juice= 4 net carbs; 3 tbsp. of cream = 0 net carbs; 2 tbsp. of chopped onion = 1g net carb.

Total Net Carbs= 11.4g

YUMMY SUMMER SQUASH AND ZUCCHINI SOUP

INGREDIENTS:

2 tablespoons butter

1 cup diced onion

2 large summer squash, peeled and cut into 1-inch cubes

1 medium sized zucchini sliced and diced

6 cups homemade (if possible) chicken stock or broth

Salt and pepper to taste

1-2 teaspoon curry powder, to taste (optional)

2 tbsp. of 35% heavy cream

PREPARATION:

Add onion to a large stock pot over medium low heat and sauté in 2 tbsp. butter stirring occasionally, until onion is soft.

Add squash and zucchini chicken stock and bring to a boil.

Reduce heat, cover and simmer for 20-30 minutes, or until squash is tender.

Puree in your regular blender, in batches, carefully venting the lid.

Return to pot.

Taste for seasoning and add salt and pepper, if necessary.

Stir in curry powder.

Simmer for 5 more minutes. into bowls and serve with a drizzle of heavy cream.

Spoon into bowls

Nutritional Information: 10 Net Carb/2 cup serving

CREAM OF MUSHROOM SOUP

INGREDIENTS:

¼ cup butter

½ cup chopped onion

1 pound of chopped fresh mushrooms

¼ cup almond flour

Salt and pepper to taste

Garlic powder-or 1 clove, minced

2 cups beef stock

1 cup 35% heavy cream

1 cup unsweetened almond milk

PREPARATION:

Put butter, onions and mushrooms in a large pot.

Sauté until onion is soft and clear.

Add flour, salt, pepper and garlic.

Mix in.

Stir in beef stock and milk.

Heat and Stir until it boils and thickens.

Stir in cream.

Bring to boiling temperature and serve.

Makes about 5 cups.

Nutritional Information: 6g. Net Carb/1 cup serving

DID U KNOW?

MUSHROOMS

A daily serving of mushrooms helps women lose belly fat. The polysaccharides in mushrooms help block fat formation and revs up your metabolic rate. They're the only veggie with vitamin D – and people who get the most tend to have the least flab.

ZUCCHINI SOUP

INGREDIENTS:

2 pounds zucchini, sliced, unpeeled

1 medium onion, sliced

1 garlic clove minced

1 tbsp. butter

2 cups hot water

2 chicken bouillon cubes

½ tsp. lemon juice

1 tsp. salt

1 tbsp. chopped chives

PREPARATION:

Combine zucchini, onion garlic and butter in the frying pan.

Sauté slowly while covered to (steam-fry) until soft-8-10 minutes.

Add water, chicken bouillon cubes, lemon juice and salt.

Run through blender

Return to saucepan.

Heat

Stir in chives.

Makes 5 cups.

Optional- ½ tsp. curry powder.

Nutritional Information: 7 Net Carbs/1 cup serving

MAIN DISH RECIPES

DINNER

CREAMY BEEF/ CHICKEN/ PORK DISH

INGREDIENTS:

12 asparagus spears (tough ends broken off) chopped in 1 ½ inch pieces

4-5 chopped white mushrooms

½ of a red bell pepper chopped in ¾" pieces

½ of a small onion chopped in small pieces

2 chicken breasts sliced into bite size pieces or 12 ounce beef or 12 ounce pork, or bag of shrimp (or a mixture of any of these)

3 tbsp. extra virgin olive oil or coconut oil

1-3 tablespoons of Worcestershire sauce

¼ cup of crumbled feta cheese or 2 tbsp. Philadelphia roasted red pepper cream cheese

¼ cup of 35% whipping cream- 0 carbs

1 egg

Keg steak spice

Italian seasoning to taste

Granulated onion powder to taste

Optional - 2 strips of bacon chopped into ¼" pieces

- Garlic powder or 2 fresh garlic cloves

- ½ tsp. chilli peppers (optional)

PREPARATION:

Combine veggies and oil along with the onions in a frying pan on medium low heat (if using bacon then add it in with the veggies) and season to taste.

Mix in 1-3 tbsp. of Worcestershire sauce

Add meat after a couple of minutes and fry until cooked.

Blend in feta cheese or cream cheese

Beat egg into cream. When feta cheese is melted stir in the egg/ cream mixture

Simmer for two minutes

Makes 2 servings

*The beauty of this dish is that it can be made with any non-starch vegetables such as broccoli, cauliflower, mushrooms spinach etc.

Nutritional Information: Approximately 6 grams of carbs/serving, (8 if using cream cheese)

Adjust your veggie amounts according to the amount of meat you are making.

CHICKEN TOPPED WITH BROCCOLI AND CAULIFLOWER

INGREDIENTS:

1 cup (500 ml) small broccoli florets or cauliflower (1 floret = 0.4 net carb)

2 chicken breasts with skin

¼ tsp. (1 ml) each of salt and pepper

¼ cup mayonnaise style dressing

1 tbsp. prepared mustard

1 onion finely chopped

½ cup cheddar cheese, divided

2 tbsp. (30 ml) sliced almonds

PREPARATION:

Preheat oven to 375° Blanch the broccoli in boiling salted water for 3 minutes. Drain and rinse under cold running water. Reserve

Arrange chicken on a foil-lined baking sheet and season with salt and pepper

Combine mayonnaise dressing and mustard and stir in the broccoli, onion and ¼ cup (125) ml) of the cheese

Spread an equal amount of the mixture evenly onto each chicken breast.

Bake for 15-17 minutes (or until internal temperature reaches 165°F/74°C

Sprinkle with the remaining cheese and almonds.

Broil for 1-2 minutes or until almonds are lightly brown and cheese is bubbly.

Nutritional Information: For one chicken breast = 2 g Net Carbs

LUSCIOUS PORK CHOPS AND CAULIFLOWER FLORETS WITH CHEESE SAUCE

INGREDIENTS:

2-3 Pork Chops or how many you need for supper

In the morning season each pork chop liberally with Montreal Steak spice, parsley and paprika and rub in.

Set aside in fridge for the day.

½ onion

3 tbsp. extra virgin olive oil

PREPARATION:

Coarsely chop ½ onion

Measure 3 tbsp. of extra virgin olive oil into frying pan

Place chopped onions in frying pan with the extra virgin olive oil and fry until onions are golden brown

Add pork chops

In separate pot filled with water boil a head of cauliflower until it reaches your desired texture.

CHEESE SAUCE

INGREDIENTS:

1 cup of 35% cream

1 egg

2 slices of your favourite cheese

Salt and pepper seasoned to your taste

PREPARATION:

Mix together the 1 cup of cream and egg.

Heat this mixture in a pot on stove then add the slices of cheese and seasonings.

Simmer until all ingredients are well blended.

Pour over cauliflower

Serves 2-3 as a side dish.

Nutritional Information: Cauliflower florets are 1 net carb each

1 large Pork Chop = 0 net carbs

Cheese sauce = 4 net carbs (depending on what kind of cheese slice you use).

Nutritional Information: Net Carb = 4-6g

DID U KNOW?

pH OF YOUR STOMACH

By closely matching the stomach's pH, citric acid helps maintain the body's acid-alkaline balance by aiding digestion without stimulating excess acid production.

FAST AND TANGY BEEF KEBABS- ALKALINIZING SUPER-MEAL:

INGREDIENTS:

½ cup balsamic vinaigrette

1 tbsp. each lemon juice, Dijon mustard, minced thyme and rosemary

1 tsp. lemon zest

2 zucchini halved and sliced

2 orange, red, yellow or green peppers cut into 2 inch cubes

1 red onion cut into wedges

4 white mushrooms chopped into large pieces

1½ pound boneless beef sirloin, cubed

6 skewers

PREPARATION:

Blend first 7 ingredients in a bowl

Place the veggies, beef and ½ of the herb mixture in a plastic bag; marinate 30 minutes.

Remove veggies, beef and meat and throw out the bag.

Thread meat and veggies unto water-soaked skewers.

Grill kebabs on heated grill for 8-10 minutes and baste with rest of the herb mixture

Nutritional information: Protein=30g. Carbs=8g. Fiber =2g. Total fat=11g. Net Carbs=6g/skewer

FRIED CAULIFLOWER

INGREDIENTS:

2 - 3 small heads of cauliflower (or 1 large)

2 tablespoons of extra virgin olive oil

¼ tsp. of sea salt

1 clove garlic, minced

1 small bunch of chives, chopped

Zest of one lemon

Freshly grated Parmesan

PREPARATION:

Cut cauliflower into tiny florets making sure the pieces are relatively equal in size, so they cook in the same amount of time.

Rinse under running water, and set aside.

Heat the extra virgin olive oil and sea salt in a large skillet over medium-high heat.

Add the cauliflower when hot and stir until the florets are coated.

Wait until the florets get a bit brown on the bottom,

Toss the cauliflower with a spatula.

Brown a bit more and continue to sauté until the pieces are deeply golden - about six minutes.

Remove from heat and stir in the chives, lemon zest, and sprinkle with a bit of freshly grated Parmesan cheese and in the last 30 seconds stir in the garlic.

Serve immediately.

Serves 2-3 as a side.

Nutritional Information: Each medium size floret is 1.0 net carbs.

HERBED PORK MEDALLIONS

INGREDIENTS:

1-1/2 pounds pork tenderloin

2 tbsp. butter, melted

¼ tsp. garlic powder

½ tsp. sea salt

½ tsp. dried tarragon

½ tsp. dried thyme

1/8 tsp. pepper

¼ tsp. cayenne pepper

PREPARATION:

Cut pork into 1 inch slices and pound to flatten.

Combine butter and garlic powder

Brush over pork

Mix seasonings together

Sprinkle over pork.

Place into greased baking pans.

Broil 4-6 inches from the heat for 5 minutes.

Turn and broil 3 minutes

Serves 6.

Nutritional Information: 0 Net Carbs

VINAIGRETTE VEGETABLES

INGREDIENTS:

3 cups fresh broccoli florets

1 medium zucchini

½ cup sweet yellow, green or red pepper

3 tablespoons of Extra Virgin Olive Oil

4-5 tsp. red wine vinegar or cider vinegar

1 garlic clove-minced

½ tsp. sea salt

¼ tsp. dried thyme

PREPARATION:

Place broccoli in a steamer basket then put in a saucepan with over 1 inch of water.

Bring to a boil

Cover and steam for 5 minutes.

Add zucchini and yellow, red or green pepper

Cover and steam for 2 minutes or until vegetables are tender crisp.

Combine in a jar with a tight-fitting lid, the oil, vinegar, garlic, salt and thyme.

Shake Well

Transfer veggies to a bowl

Add dressing and toss to coat.

Nutritional Information: 6g. Net Carbs/1 cup serving serving

PORK AND ASPARAGUS STIR-FRY

INGREDIENTS:

8 oz. (225g) pork loin chops cut into strips

2 tbsp. almond flour

1 tsp. soy sauce

1 tsp. grated ginger

1 pound asparagus, trimmed

2 tbsp. extra virgin olive oil or coconut oil

3 green onions cut in 1 ½ inch pieces.

1 cup sliced white mushrooms

½ cup chicken broth

PREPARATION:

Toss together pork, soy sauce, almond flour and ginger to coat.

Set aside.

Cut each asparagus stalk into 4 pieces.

Set aside.

Heat oil over high heat in a wok.

Stir-fry green onions, about 30 seconds.

Add pork and fry until no longer pink, about 1 minute.

Mix in asparagus and mushrooms, stir-fry for 1 minute.

Stir in chicken broth.

Stir fry until asparagus is tender-crisp, 1-2 minutes.

Makes 4 servings

Nutritional Information: 8g carbs; 3g fiber; 5g net carbs.

HAVE YOUR BREAD AND EAT IT TOO!

BREAD MACHINE LOW CARB BREAD AND PIZZA DOUGH

INGREDIENTS:

Dough	Medium Pizza Dough	Large Pizza Dough
35% Cream- 80°-90°F (27°-32° C)	1 ¾ cups (425ml)	2 cups (375ml)
Salt	½ tsp. (2ml)	¾ tsp. (4ml)
Whole Wheat Flour	1 cup (250ml)	1 ¼ cups (300ml)
Vital Wheat Gluten	½ cup (125ml)	2/3 cup (150ml
Barley Flour	½ cup (125ml)	2/3 cup (150ml)
Almond Flour	½ cup (125ml)	2/3 cup (150ml)
Soy Protein	2 tbsps. (30ml)	2 ½ tbsps. (37ml)
Flax seed	2 tbsps. (30ml)	2 ½ tbsps. (37ml)
Yeast, active dry, instant or	2 ¼ tsps. (11ml)	2 ¼ tsps. (11ml)
Bread machine: Nutritional Information: Per Serving-Carbs = 7g; Protein- 4g; Fiber-1g; Net Carb=6g.		

PREPARATION:

Place ingredients in the order listed in the bread pan and chose the pizza dough cycle.

IF YOU DON'T OWN A BREAD MACHINE YOU CAN STILL MAKE THIS RECIPE BY HAND.

HANDMADE PREPARATION:

Blend all ingredients together.

Turn dough out onto floured board and knead, adding small spoonfuls of flour if needed, until the dough is soft and smooth, not sticky to the touch.

Put dough in bowl.

Cover and let rise in warm spot for 1 hour.

Punch down dough.

Turn out onto floured board and knead.

Let rise for another ½ hour in bowl

Preheat oven at 375 degrees F.

Form dough into loaf and set in bread pan.

Cover and let rise for about 30 minutes.

Score dough by cutting three slashes across the top with a sharp knife.

Put in oven and bake for about 45 minutes or until golden brown.

Turn out bread and let cool on a rack or clean dish towel.

*For pizza dough just let the dough rise once, punch down then roll out onto pizza pan.

TOPPINGS:

You can mix ½ cup of mild or medium salsa with ¼ cup sugarless tomato sauce.

Grated cheese, bacon bits, mushrooms, sliced pepperoni and chopped green peppers.

Pre-heat oven and bake at 400°F for 20 minutes.

Nutritional Information: Each serving of pizza= 8-10g of net carbs.

DID U KNOW?

NUTRITIVE VALUES OF GREEN BELL PEPPER, PER 100 G

Vitamin A; 630 I.U.

Vitamin B; Thiamine .04 mg.

Vitamin C; 120 mg.

Calcium; 11 mg.

Phosphorus; 25 mg.

Potassium; 170 gm.

Carbohydrates; 2.4 gm.

Protein ; 1.2 gm.

Calories ; 25

Bell peppers are not only an excellent source of carotenoids, but also a source of over 30 different members of the carotenoid nutrient family. When you consume bell peppers, your body converts beta-carotene into retinol, one of the most usable and active forms of vitamin A. Together with vitamin C, vitamin A counteracts free radicals so as to minimize the damage caused to your arteries, nerves and tissues.

If you need to replenish vitamin C, consider eating red or yellow bell peppers as they provide 3 to 4 times more vitamin C than the daily recommended value. In fact, a green bell pepper contains twice as much vitamin C as an orange.

ASPARAGUS PIZZA

INGREDIENTS:

1 low carb pizza dough

¼ cup extra virgin olive oil

Pepper to taste

2 minced garlic cloves

1 cup shredded Mozzarella cheese (or your preference of cheese).

¼ cup grated Parmesan or Romano cheese

PREPARATION:

Pre-heat oven to 425°F

Stretch and roll low carb pizza dough over a 16 by 12 inch, cornmeal dusted pizza pan.

Cover with a tea towel and leave for 20 minutes while the dough rises a little. (You can skip this step if you prefer a thin crust).

Mix the asparagus in a large bowl with

Half of the oil and

Season with salt and pepper to taste

Set Aside

Stir remaining oil with garlic and spread over the dough.

Top with asparagus, Mozzarella, Romano/Parmesan cheese.

Bake in oven until crust is golden brown-about 20 minutes.

Makes 8-10 slices

Nutritional Information: 1 cup mozzarella=4.3g net carbs, 1 slice low carb pizza crust= 5g. Net Carbs

DID U KNOW?

ASPARAGUS is an alkaline food which is rich in protein but low in calories and carbohydrates. It is an excellent source of potassium, folic acid, vitamins A, C, K, and traces of vitamin B complex. Asparagus has an abundance of an amino acid called asparagine, which helps to cleanse the body of waste material. As a result, some people pass out smelly urine after eating asparagus.

A good source of dietary fiber, asparagus is also rich in niacin, phosphorus and very low in sodium. Certainly most impressive, is that it is one of those few vegetables that actually has the calcium and magnesium in the ideal ratio of 2:1. The diuretic and alkaline properties of asparagus help prevent or dissolve kidney stones. It helps break up oxalic acid crystals formed in the kidney. The anti-oxidant and glutathione in asparagus prevents the progression of cataracts and other eye problems.

PESTO- PARMESAN TOPPER

INGREDIENTS:

1- 3 ounce chicken breast

2 tbsp. basil

1 tbsp. finely grated parmesan cheese

2 tsp. toasted pine nuts

1 tsp. extra virgin olive oil

½ tsp. finely shredded lemon peel

1 small clove of garlic, minced

PREPARATION:

1) **Sauté** or grill chicken breast until cooked through

2) **Combine** in a small bowl basil, cheese, pine nuts, oil, lemon peel and garlic.

3) **Spoon** topping over warm chicken breast.

Serves 1

Nutritional Information: Net Carbs= 2g.

BACON-WRAPPED MINI MEATLOAF

INGREDIENTS:

1 tsp. extra virgin olive oil

½ cup grated carrots = 4 net carbs

½ onion, finely chopped

1 garlic clove, minced

½ pound minced turkey

1 egg, lightly beaten

¼ cup finely chopped parsley

¼ cup finely grated parmesan or romano cheese

2 tbsp. mild or medium salsa

4 strips of 0 carb bacon

PREPARATION:

Heat oil in a large non-stick pan over medium heat

Cook carrots and onion until tender and golden-5 minutes.

Set aside to cool

Combine in a bowl, using your hands, the turkey, egg, parsley, garlic and grated cheese.

Mix in the salsa, and cooled carrot, onion mixture until just blended

Do not knead the mixture together too much since it will become tough when cooked.

Divide into 4 equal portions

Shape each patty

Wrap a slice of bacon around the edge of each patty.

***You can freeze these individual patties in plastic wrap and store in re-sealable plastic freezer bags.**

Place patties that you are going to cook on a greased cooking sheet

Bake in a preheated oven at 190°C (375°F) until each patty is cooked through-or has an internal temperature of 74°C (165°F) – 40 to 45 minutes.

Nutritional Information: Net Carbs/serving 6g.

SALMON LOAF-SLOW COOKER

INGREDIENTS:

1 ½ cups or 375ml of finely grated low carb bread crumbs. (Remember- the whiter the bread the sooner you're dead-this applies even to the bread crumbs you use!)

½ cup of unsweetened almond milk-whatever your preference

2 large fork beaten eggs

2-7.5 ounces or 2-213g of salmon –canned is perfectly acceptable-drained and liquid reserved

1 ½ tablespoons or 25ml of lemon juice-from freshly squeezed lemons if possible

1 tablespoon or 15ml onion flakes

¾ teaspoon or 4 ml of sea salt

¼ teaspoon or 1ml of pepper

PREPARATION:

Blend eggs with reserved liquid from salmon, lemon juice, onion flakes, salt and pepper along with the milk in a large bowl. Stir in the bread crumbs.

Flake the salmon and stir into the bread crumb mixture.

Pack into a greased (with extra virgin olive oil) 3 ½ quart (3.5 liters) slow cooker. Leave some room so the side of the mixture does not touch the sides of the slow cooker.

Cover and cook on low for 4-5 hours, high for 2-2 ½ hours.

Nutritional Information: 15 oz. of salmon is 0 net carbs and also packs a whopping 73.1g of protein and 22.3g of fat.

CREAM SAUCE

Combine in a small bowl-:

¾ cup 35% heavy cream

2 tablespoons of chopped scallions or fresh chives

2 tablespoons chopped parsley

1 garlic clove, minced

1 ½ teaspoon of fresh lemon juice

1 ½ teaspoon of white wine vinegar

1/8 teaspoon of black pepper

Stir gently all 7 ingredients until well blended

Cover and refrigerate until required.

PS: As an extra benefit you can thinly slice the leftovers from the loaf for sandwiches the next day.

Nutritional Information: 0 Net Carbs/serving

DID U KNOW?

OMEGA 3

♥Omega 3 is associated with reduced body inflammation. The Omega 3 in Salmon, besides being the top anti-inflammatory food, helps to improve brain function. Salmon is not high in saturated fat.

♥Omega-3 fatty acids benefit the heart of healthy people, and those at high risk of — or who already have cardiovascular disease.

♥Research has shown that Omega-3 fatty acids decrease the risk of arrhythmias (abnormal heartbeats).

♥Omega-3 fatty acids also decrease triglyceride levels, slow growth rates of atherosclerotic plaque, and help lower blood pressure when consumed consistently.

GRILLED SALMON WITH TOMATO SALSA

INGREDIENTS:

1 cup tomato salsa-optional-mild or medium

2/3 cup (150 mL) green onions, sliced

6 tbsp. (90 mL) chopped fresh cilantro, divided

2 tsp. (10 mL) seeded jalapeno pepper (optional), finely chopped

4 tbsp. (60 mL) butter

6 Salmon fillets, (about 1 1/2 lbs. or 750 g)

PREPARATION:

Combine tomato salsa, green onions, 4 tablespoons cilantro and jalapeno pepper in a large bowl; set aside.

Blend butter with remaining 2 tablespoons cilantro in a small bowl.

Grill or broil salmon, brushing with cilantro spread, 15 minutes or until salmon is done.

Serve salsa with salmon.

Nutritional Information: Fat-19 grams; Carbs- 6 grams; Fiber 1.9grams; Net Carbs=4.1grams

MORE DID U KNOW ON OMEGA 3?

BELLY BURNER!

Fish is high in Omega 3 fatty acids. Omega 3's set belly fat on fire! Omega 3 fatty acids activate ab-fat melting enzymes during exercise. Omega 3's not only play a vital role in the health of the membrane of every cell in our body, they also helps protect us from a number of key health threats.

In one study completed by an Australian researcher, walkers were given extra Omega 3's. They shed 5% of their belly fat. Walkers not given Omega 3's lost none. It is recommended to have 1-2 servings of Omega 3 rich food daily like fish such as salmon, trout, herring, swordfish, cod, blue fish and mackerel, Canola and Soybean oils and nuts such as walnuts, pecans and pine nuts, flaxseed oil and omega-3 eggs.

The benefits of omega-3s include reducing the risk of heart disease and stroke while helping to reduce symptoms of hypertension, depression, attention deficit hyperactivity disorder (ADHD), joint pain and other rheumatoid problems, as well as certain skin ailments. Omega 3's help reduce inflammation throughout your body. Some research has even shown that omega-3s can boost the immune system and help protect us from an array of illnesses including Alzheimer's disease.

Omega 3 improves the body's ability to respond to insulin by stimulating the secretion of leptin, a hormone that helps regulate food intake, body weight and metabolism.

GRILLED VEGETABLE PLATTER

INGREDIENTS:

4 each sweet red and orange peppers

4 each yellow and green zucchinis

2 small red onions

9 white mushrooms

½ cup extra virgin olive oil

¼ tsp. each of salt and pepper

PREPARATION:

Core and seed red and orange peppers and cut into quarters

Cut zucchinis lengthwise into ¼ inch thick strips

Cut onions into ½ inch thick rings

Remove stems from mushrooms

Brush vegetables with extra virgin olive oil, salt and pepper.

Place on greased grill over medium high heat

Close lid and grill, turning once.

Grill until tender and lightly charred – 10-15 minutes

Makes 12 servings.

Nutritional Information: 14g of carbs; 4g of fiber; 10g net carbs/ serving.

SERVE WITH THIS TASTY 0 NET CARB DIP

INGREDIENTS:

1 cup packed fresh parsley leaves

2 tbsp. packed fresh oregano leaves

2 cloves garlic

½ seeded jalapeno pepper

¼ tsp. each of sea salt and pepper

¼ cup extra virgin olive oil

2tbsp. water

1 tbsp. red wine vinegar

PREPARATION:

Finely chop together in a food processor the parsley, oregano, garlic, jalapeno pepper.

Add into the food processor the extra virgin olive oil, water and vinegar.

Pulse until combined

Makes ½ cup.

1g. carb; 1g fiber; 0 Net Carb

DECADENT DESSERTS

DESSERTS

STRAWBERRY/BLUEBERRY ICE CREAM

Measure ½ cup of strawberries or blueberries

1 cup 35% cream (make sure it is 0 carbs)

1-2 tbsp. stevia or Splenda

1 tsp. cinnamon

Place in freezer for 30 minutes

NO-BAKE BLUEBERRY AND STRAWBER

INGREDIENTS:

1 cup boiling water

1 box sugar-free strawberry jello

1 cup 35% whipping cream

1 (8 ounce) package Philadelphia Cream Cheese

1 cup sucralose or your preferred sweetener

1 cup blueberries (fresh or frozen)

1 cup strawberries (fresh or frozen)

FILLING:

In a small bowl, dissolve Jello in the boiling water, stirring for 2-3 minutes. Place in fridge to partially set.

NEXT: In a bowl, beat whipping cream and set aside in fridge.

Beat the cream cheese in a large bowl with ½ cup sweetener until smooth.

Mix in partially set strawberry jello.

Fold in whipping cream along with the cup of strawberries and blueberries.

Pour into pie pan

Chill 2-3 hours.

Nutritional Information: Makes 8 slices with each slice = 2 net carbs.

This dessert can also be made as custard using the lime, peach, cherry or orange gelatine.

HOMEMADE PEANUT BUTTER

You can make your own peanut butter in a Vita-Mix blender.

INGREDIENTS:

4 ½ cups peanuts= 11.9 net carbs

3 tbsps. Extra Virgin Olive Oil= 0 net carbs

PEANUT BUTTER COOKIES – YES YOU CAN HAVE COOKIES!!!

INGREDIENTS:

1 cup of natural sugar-free peanut butter

1 egg

¼ cup of sweetener (your preference, optional)

¼ cup almond meal/flour

PREPARATION:

Pre-heat oven to 325°F

Mix 1 cup of peanut butter with the egg and sweetener (if desired) until well blended.

Add the almond flour

Roll into 12 balls

Place 2 inches apart on a well-greased baking sheet.

Flatten with a fork.

Bake 15 minutes or until lightly browned.

Makes 1 dozen cookies.

Nutritional Information: 1 cup peanut butter= 11.9 net carbs; <u>each cookie is a little less than 1g of net carb.</u>

CHOCOLATE CLOUD PUFFS

INGREDIENTS:

3 egg whites

1 tbsp. cocoa

¼ cup Splenda

PREPARATION:

Preheat oven to 200°C.

Whip egg whites in a bowl until they form stiff peaks.

Fold in a tablespoon of cocoa carefully

Add 1/4 cup of Splenda.

Place spoonfuls onto a cookie sheet and bake for a half-hour at 200 degrees.

Let them cool down and dry out thoroughly.

Nutritional Information: Less than 1g Net Carbs/ serving.

PANNA COTTA

Panna cotta is a classic Italian dessert of molded custard made with cream and gelatine typically served with strawberries.

INGREDIENTS:

1 Tbsp (or 15 ml) powdered gelatine (can be any flavour)

2 oz. of ice cold water

12 oz. 35% whipping cream (no carb)

4 oz. Splenda or Stevia

1 oz. of 2% fat buttermilk

Pinch of salt

PREPARATION:

Sprinkle gelatine over cold water.

Combine cream, sweetener (of choice) and salt in a microwave-safe bowl

Heat the cream mixture until warm and the sweetener has dissolved

Heat the gelatine until it has just melted.

Avoid boiling the gelatine.

Mix the gelatine and the cream and stir well until completely incorporated.

Stir in the buttermilk

Divide the panna cotta into individual serving glasses

Nutritional Information: 1-2g Net Carb/serving

DID U KNOW?

NATURAL PEANUT BUTTER

The fiber provided by peanuts is known to aid with the digestion process. The health benefits of peanuts are also augmented by the presence of vitamins D and E.

Peanut butter contains high amounts of proteins--as much as 24 percent by weight. Along with protein, peanut butter contains vitamins E and B3 and the minerals copper and iron. It also contains calcium and potassium.

Raw peanut butter seems to have even more beneficial effects, because the peanut butter is typically made with the crushed skins of the peanuts, and consequently contains more minerals. The iron contained in peanut butter is critical for the functioning of the red blood cells in the body, and calcium contained in peanut butter contributes to healthy bones.

CHAPTER 10
SUPPLEMENTS

CHAPTER 10

THE FOLLOWING ARE THE SUPPLEMENTS WE RECOMMEND WHILE YOU ARE ON THE SERIAL KILLER DIET THAT HAVE ALL PROVEN TO REDUCE CORTISOL AND INSULIN:

1) Vitamin D3

2) Magnesium

3) Navitol

4) Omega 3

5) Probiotics

1) VITAMIN D3

We at the Martin Clinic have accumulated over 300 studies that confirm Vitamin D3 is the most essential of all vitamins. According to the Journal of Clinical Nutrition taking 2000 I.U. of Vitamin D daily can reduce the risk of developing:

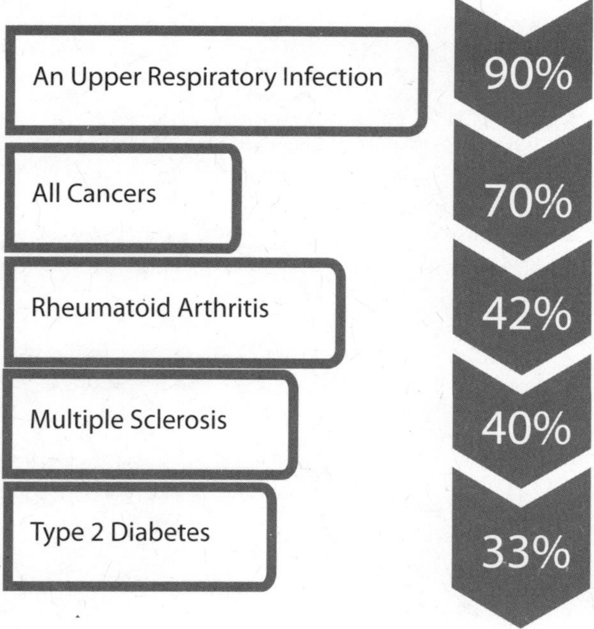

IF ANY DRUG COULD PROMISE THESE KINDS OF RESULTS THE DRUG COMPANY WOULD BECOME THE BIGGEST CORPORATION IN THE WORLD!

For our purposes I want to concentrate on Vitamin D3 and its relationship to cortisol and insulin. There is a link between low levels of Vitamin D3 and autism, schizophrenia, diabetes, kidney health, cancer, depression and heart disease. All of these disorders have a cortisol and insulin component.

Scientists have uncovered the ultimate catch 22:

1) Circulating Vitamin D3 is associated with fast and easy fat burn. This is due to Vitamin D3 helping cells with insulin resistance and aiding in the regulation of the pancreas.

2) Fat cells lock up Vitamin D3 creating a lack of the nutrient in virtually 100% of obese women.

Women with insufficient Vitamin D levels had 80% more abdominal fat than their high level Vitamin D peers.

Vitamin D3 acts like a hormone in the body according to James E Dowel MD., co-author of the "Vitamin D Cure". Therefore a deficiency can cause all sorts of symptoms such as:

1) Chronic Inflammation

2) Foggy thinking

3) High blood pressure

4) Frequent body aches

5) Restless sleep

We at the Martin Clinic recommend for adults 5,000 I.U. of Vitamin D3 for the months of September through May if you live in the Northern Hemisphere. If you live in the sunny south of the USA and you sunbathe at least 3-4 times a week for ½ hour with no sunscreen or sunblock you might not have to supplement with Vitamin D3. However if you have dark skin you absolutely need to take a supplement of Vitamin D3. It's funny because when we tested several Floridians for Vitamin D3 levels last year we found most to be very deficient.

2) MAGNESIUM

"Magnesium acts like a spark plug for your adrenals and for the energy production of every cell in your body." Dr. James L. Wilson, "Adrenal Fatigue –the 21st Century Stress Syndrome".

I test for magnesium deficiency in my office and the vast majority of people I test are deficient in this essential mineral. If you have adrenal stress with high levels of cortisol you have magnesium deficiency.

Adrenal stress puts an enormous strain on your magnesium levels and without enough magnesium your sleep patterns will be disrupted.

"Think of magnesium as the relaxation mineral. Anything that is tight, crampy, irritable and stiff whether it is a body part or mood-is a sign of magnesium deficiency." Dr. Mark Hyman M.D.

Here are signs of possible magnesium deficiency:

1) Headaches-especially migraines

2) Insomnia

3) Obesity

4) Heart palpitation

5) Behavioural disorders, i.e.: ADD, ADHD, autism

6) Irritability

7) Constipation

8) CFS and Fibromyalgia

9) Asthma

10) Kidney stones

11) Diabetes, (Hypoglycemia – low blood sugar)

12) Obesity

13) Osteoporosis

14) Acid reflux

15) Trouble swallowing

BEST SOURCE OF MAGNESIUM IN FOODS

1) Kelp-sea vegetable

2) Almonds

3) Nuts (not peanut butter)

4) Wheat bran, wheat germ, rye flour

5) Greens-broccoli, spinach

6) Beans

High levels of magnesium are associated with 40% decrease in cardiovascular deaths.

I often recommend to my Chronic Fatigue and Fibromyalgia patients to take hot baths several times a week with Epsom salts so the magnesium is absorbed right through the skin!!

What decreases magnesium levels in the body?

1) High stress

2) Alcohol

3) Blood pressure medication

4) Table salt

5) Sodas

6) Yeast, parasites

We at the Martin Clinic recommend 400-1000mg of magnesium citrate daily.

3) NAVITOL-PINE BARK EXTRACT

I wrote a book in the 1990's called Pine Bark Extract- The Bark with the Bite. We at the Martin Clinic discovered the #1 positive effect of Pine Bark. It gives you energy! If you have low energy and are running on fumes you absolutely need to be taking this supplement.

> According to Clinical diabetes studies scientists discovered that type 2 diabetes patients had lower blood sugar and healthier blood vessels after supplementing with Pine Bark Extract. Diabetes Care March, 2004 Issue

I had discovered that Navitol was the only supplement that consistently helped my patients who suffered from Chronic Fatigue Syndrome and Fibromyalgia.

MAJOR BENEFITS OF NAVITOL

1) Reduces adrenal stress

2) Increases circulation

3) Reduces blood pressure

4) Reduces insulin secretion by slowing sugar uptake

5) Reduces cortisol secretion

6) Increases collagen levels in the skin promoting healthy skin and decreasing wrinkles.

7) Crosses the blood brain barrier to increase oxygen to the brain.

8) Protects the body against harmful UVA radiation (the skin cancer-bad radiation)

9) Protects against free radicals.

10) Reduces edema.

11) Helpful to reduce varicose veins.

12) Effective for treating Diabetic Retinopathy and Macular Degeneration.

13) Reduces symptoms of PMS and Endometriosis.

14) Increases memory and reduces risk of Alzheimers and Dementia

15) Effective treatment for ADD, ADHD or any other behavioural conditions.

16) Tremendous natural anti-inflammatory-a Cox-2 inhibitor.

17) Pine Bark is as effective as aspirin in anti-platelet aggregation with no side effects.

4) OMEGA 3

There is so much research as to the benefits of Omega 3 I don't know where to start. However, I want to concentrate primarily on Omega 3's part in reducing insulin and cortisol.

Omega 3 fatty acids protect cell membranes, Remember, over 50% of the body's cell walls are comprised of fat. Omega 3 is essential for insulin receptors on the cell wall to function properly. Earlier in the book I talked about how insulin is like a key that opens a cell wall. If you have insulin resistance the key (insulin) has trouble opening the cell wall to allow sugar to enter the cell. Think of Omega 3 like WD-40 that helps to open up the jammed lock.

ANIMAL KINGDOM SOURCES OMEGA 3	PLANT KINGDOM OMEGA 3
Fish oil, sardines, cod, halibut, macherel, herring	Flax seeds
Grass fed beef	Hemp seed
	Nuts, seeds

5) PROBIOTICS

At one time the food we ate used to be grown in nutrient rich, unpolluted soil. Beneficial soil and plant based probiotic microbes used to be ingested because of this soil.

However, for the last 1/2 century we have been sterilizing our soil with pesticides and herbicides, destroying most bacteria both bad and good. Our modern lifestyle, which includes antibiotic drug use, chlorinated water, chemical ingestion, pollution and poor diet (fast food), is responsible for eradicating much of the beneficial bacteria in our bodies. A lack of beneficial probiotic microbes often results in poor intestinal and immune system health. Many symptoms may result from a lack of probiotics.

NOT ALL PROBIOTIC IS CREATED EQUAL SO THE MARTIN CLINIC PROBIOTIC contains 14 different strains of bacteria (the most powerful probiotic on the market) which gives one complete coverage from sinuses to the reproductive organs.

These probiotics are designed to resist chlorine, fluorine, ascorbic acid, hydrochloric acid, heat, cold, and extremes of pH. These probiotics cannot be destroyed the way ordinary probiotics are.

Seventy to eighty percent of your immune system is in the stomach and digestive tract and when it isn't working as it should you are open to all kinds of illness and disease.

Our unique high potency multi-stain, friendly bacteria successfully survive stomach acids and reach the intestinal tract. These friendly bacteria multiply and re-populate along the length of the intestinal tract and this increases our ability to both absorb and assimilate nutrients from our food.

Surprising new Canadian research shows that 90% of the calming serotonin in your bloodstream isn't made by your brain cells-it is made by the healthy probiotic bacteria living in your digestive tract!

Since our Probiotic is plant –based it does not need to be refrigerated, even after it is opened!

SOME OF THE MANY USES OF PROBIOTICS:

– Stops intestinal gas before it starts.

– Helps keep the digestive system regular.

– Research has proven that the more healthy friendly bacteria that reside in your digestive tract, the more stronger your immune system is in stopping harmful stuff from entering your system.

Bacteria have a reputation for causing disease, so the idea of tossing down a few billion a day for your health might seem — literally and figuratively — hard to swallow.

BUT, a growing body of scientific evidence suggests that you can treat and even prevent some illnesses with foods and supplements containing certain kinds of live bacteria.

Some digestive disease specialists are recommending them for disorders that frustrate conventional medicine, such as irritable bowel syndrome, diarrhea and Crohn's disease.

British researchers stated that a study showed that probiotic, or "good" bacteria can change the immune system's response…and balance antibodies in a way that can provide relief to people with allergy symptoms.

Friendly bacteria (probiotics), also help to manufacture many vitamins including the B-complex vitamins, folic acid, vitamin A and vitamin K.

They can also out-compete "bad bacteria" that may cause disease.

CHAPTER 11

MARTIN CLINIC

LEADER IN PREVENTATIVE MEDICINE FOR 100 YEARS

1911 – 2011

CHAPTER 11

HISTORY OF THE MARTIN CLINIC

In 1911 my grandfather David Martin founded the Martin clinic in Timmins Ontario, Canada. My grandfather died the same year that I was born, in 1952. However, my grandfather's exploits in health care were legendary. In French (I am a French Canadian) David Martin was said to have a "don" – a gift. He was truly gifted and was light years ahead of his time in preventative medicine.

MY PERSONAL HERO

My father and my personal hero A.F. Martin was also highly recognized in alternative therapy. My father passed away in 2005 at the age of 80. Right to the very end he was still seeing patients.

There are several doctors in our family continuing the tradition of the Martin Clinic. These include my son - Dr. A.P. Martin, my brother – Dr. Peter Martin and my nephew – Dr. Shawn Martin.

THE MARTIN CLINIC PROTOCOL

After years of researching Chronic Fatigue Syndrome and Fibromyalgia, our team of researchers, have developed a unique way of testing patients to get at the root of their health problems.

THREE TIMES A YEAR

Did you know that we get brand new blood three times a year? Yes, three times a year (every four months) your blood cells are completely regenerated. Why is this significant? Well if you are still breathing there is still hope to come back from whatever your present condition may be!

We at Martin Clinic know the importance of blood when it comes to diagnosing and treating patients. We therefore use what is called "Live blood testing" using a very powerful microscope.

QUESTIONNAIRE – YOU KNOW YOU HAVE A HIGH CORTISOL LEVEL IF YOU ANSWER YES TO THREE OR MORE OF THESE QUESTIONS

	YES	NO
1) You are running on fumes and tired all of the time		
2) Brain fog		
3) Insomnia		
4) Weight gain-especially around the belly		
5) Anxiety or depression		
6) Hair loss		
7) Acne		
8) Dizziness when standing		
9) Nausea, vomiting, diarrhea		
10) Loss of appetite		
11) Craving salt or sugar-or both		
12) Extra effort to perform daily tasks		
13) Poor immunity		
14) Reliance on stimulants like coffee to get going		
15) Intolerance to cold		
16) Feeling overwhelmed or crying		
17) Feeling tired in the morning even though you have had plenty of sleep		

QUESTIONNAIRE – YOU KNOW IF YOU HAVE INSULIN RESISTANCE IF YOU ANSWER YES TO TWO OR MORE OF THESE QUESTIONS

	YES	NO
1) Do you have love handles?		
2) Fuzzy or foggy thinking		
3) Do you have a pot belly?		
4) Low energy		
5) Heartburn or acid reflux		
6) Low libido		
7) Tired after eating		
8) Mood swings		

QUESTIONNAIRE – YOU KNOW IF YOU HAVE ESTROGEN ISSUES IF YOU ANSWER YES TO TWO OR MORE OF THESE QUESTIONS

	YES	NO
1) Mental fogginess		
2) Mood swings (bossy)		
3) Trouble falling asleep at night		
4) Hot flashes		
5) Night sweats		
6) Fatigue		
7) Dry eyes, dry skin, dry vagina, loss of skin glow		
8) Bloating		
9) Heart palpitations		
10) Painful breasts		
11) Increase in breast size		
12) Water retention		
13) Pelvic cramps		

Here at the Martin clinic when someone is tired we really take a good look at their blood. Makes sense doesn't it?

Here is how my exclusive Biomarker Testing protocol can help you get MORE energy, prevent Heart Disease, avoid Cancer, Lose Weight, improve Digestion, Rid your body of Inflammation and finally return to NORMAL HEALTH.

I would like to introduce you to my exclusive Biomarker Testing protocol that formed the basis for my book: Medical Crisis – Secrets Your Doctor Won't Share With You. However, before I get into my Biomarker Testing Protocol and why I'm extremely excited about what it can do for your health, I should probably explain how I discovered this scientific breakthrough in the first place.

First of all…I've been in the health care field for a LONG time.

And, over those years I've seen and written about a CRISIS in our current health care system. When I first started in the health field, 1 out of 20 children had asthma, now it is 1 out of 3!!!! Diabetes went from being virtually unheard of to an absolute EPIDEMIC. Diseases such as ADD and ADHD were non-existent. And, don't even get me started on CANCER.

Over the past 30 years, the Medical profession has apparently done their best to stay on top of all these diseases, but let's be honest….they are too slow and too big of an entity to react to change and change is what we need.

Here's a true but unfortunate example…

It was not too long ago that the medical motto for breast cancer was "early detection is the best form of prevention". **ARE YOU KIDDING ME!** It doesn't take a nuclear physicist to figure out that if you detect something…you haven't prevented squat! A true motto should read "not having breast cancer in the first place is the best form of prevention".

You would think that the previous example of illogical thinking would be an isolated event, but in medicine it isn't. Do you want another example? How about cholesterol? There are more people today on cholesterol lowering medication and yet more than ever are dying from heart disease! Why is that? Why is it that 50% of heart attack victims have **ABSOLUTELY NORMAL** cholesterol? Yet, if you go see your doctor and he is worried about your heart, it is a STONE COLD guarantee that you are prescribed cholesterol meds!!! Are you comfortable with that? I won't even mention the ridiculous side effects.

And here lies the problem…

Let's look at the unfortunate breast cancer motto one more time. Do you know how long it takes cancer cells in the breast to grow to the size of the tip of a ball point pen? If you said 5 YEARS then I owe you a sticker! Basically what the medical profession was telling women is that by the time they "early detect" their cancer, they've already had it for 5 years! Does that sound like prevention?

One thing that I hear in my clinic EVERY DAY are stories of people who are not feeling well and have had every possible medical test done only to be told that there is nothing wrong with them. Does this make any sense? Do you know how many people have been told everything is normal, only to be diagnosed with cancer 5 years later?

Do we have any other options? Are we stuck with testing that only detects problems once YOU have them? Wouldn't it make sense if there was testing that can let you know ahead of time that your body is heading in the wrong direction? Enough is enough! There has to be another way…and there is!

MY EXCLUSIVE BIOMARKER TESTING PROTOCOL

I've been on hundreds of radio shows, television news programs and have written COUNTLESS articles on the importance of listening to very specific gauges that our body has that can warn of problems 5-10 years down the road.

These gauges, when ignored, lead to illness…it is as simple as that. Pay attention to your body's gauges and guess what? You feel better, your immune system works better, you digest better, you have more energy and…..you are practicing TRUE PREVENTION because your body is operating under ideal conditions…it is that easy!

What are these gauges? I've already told you how important they are (they can literally SAVE your life), but what are these biomarkers and how do you check them?

BIOMARKER #1 pH.

Why start with pH? Well, it's actually quite simple. Disease is allowed to grow in an acidic environment. If your pH is acidic then you are ready to host a disease. There was an article written many years ago entitled "How to raise a crook?" The purpose of the article was straight forward – if you want your child to be a crook, then you, as parents should behave a certain way. If I were to write an article entitled "How to get sick and stay that way" then my first point would be, become acidic. There is a direct correlation between acidity and disease.

BIOMARKER #2 ANTIOXIDANT PROFILE

Another key to staying healthy or restoring health is antioxidants. Take an apple and cut it in half. Leave it on the counter for a few minutes and it quickly starts to turn brown. This is oxidation or rusting in action. Take another apple and cut it in half and squirt of few drops of lemon juice on the slices and see what happens. The apple doesn't go brown quite as fast. Why? Lemon juice contains Vitamin C, which is as you know…an antioxidant. Antioxidants protect our cells from premature rusting or oxidation. Studies have shown over and over that this rusting or oxidation effect leads to cancer, diabetes, cardiovascular problems and over 60 other well-known diseases!

BIOMARKER #3 – INFLAMMATION STATUS

Here is another very important biomarker. Low grade inflammation in the body has been linked to 30% of ALL CANCERS and 100% OF HEART DISEASE!!! Did you know that you can prevent a heart attack in a patient up to 7 years ahead of time by simply testing for their inflammation status? Do you think you should have yours tested?

BIOMARKER #4 – HEAVY METAL TESTING

This important biomarker test could save you from diseases such as ALZHEIMERS, DEMENTIA and many other neurological disorders. Heavy metals have also been linked to heart disease and immune problems. If you don't think that heavy metals such as mercury are a problem for you…think again. A recent study by a former FDA scientist recently tested 20 samples of High

Fructose Corn Syrup (HFCS) and found mercury in 9 of the 20 samples!

Another researcher tested 55 common supermarket foods such as yogurt, jams; barbecue sauces and found that 1 in 3 had detectable mercury levels!!! The stuff that you are eating everyday more than likely contains mercury. And, let me tell you one thing, no amount of mercury in the body is healthy.

BIOMARKER #5 – LEAKY GUT

Eighty percent of all diseases originate in the bowel. Isn't it important therefore to test the state of your digestive tract? The Martin Clinic Biomarker Kit will do just that!!

Tests for:

- Leaky gut

- Fungus/candida

- Parasites

- Poor stomach acidity

BIOMARKER #6 – ADRENAL STRESS

Dr. Martin wrote several years ago about Adrenal stress as the major cause for Chronic Fatigue Syndrome, Fibromyalgia and belly fat.

Tests for:

- Adrenal/Cortisol testing

BIOMARKER #7 – SUGAR LEVELS

We at the Martin Clinic understand the importance of controlling blood sugar in terms of energy, weight control etc. Most doctors don't check for insulin resistance which is an important part of our biomarker testing.

Tests for:

– Urine sugar levels

– Insulin resistance

BIOMARKER #8

We also test for:

– Omega 3 levels in tissue

– Magnesium levels

– Vitamin D3

– Estrogen

– Progesterone

– B12

REFERENCES

CHAPTER 1

1) Energy Robbers and the Fatigue Cure, Dr. A. W. Martin, D.C, PhD. RNCP, DNM, Biotech Publishing, 2010

2) Adrenal Fatigue, The 21st Century Stress Syndrome, James L. Wilson, N.D., D.C., PhD. Smart Publications, 2008

3) Nutrition Reporter, March 2008, Vol. 19, #3.

4) Medical Crisis-Secrets Your Doctor Won't Share With You, Dr. A.W. Martin, Team Writers Group, 2006

5) Journal of Clinical Endocrinology and Metabolism, N.Vogelgangs, 2010

CHAPTER 2

1) American Journal of Clinical Nutrition, 2010.

2) USA Today, March 23, 2011

3) Telegraph, March 29, 2011

4) Stop Prediabetes Now, Jack Challem, John Wiley and Sons, 2007

CHAPTER 3

1) A Smart Women's Guide to Weight Loss, Lorna, R. Vanderhaeghe, M.S. Headlines Promotions Ltd.

2) Health Blog, June 11/2009

CHAPTER 4

1) Energy Robbers and the Fatigue Cure, Dr. A.W. Martin, D.C, PhD. RNCP, DNM, Biotech Publishing, 2010

2) Stop the Killing of Beneficial Bacteria, Nature, August, 2011

3) The 17 Day Diet, Dr. Mike Moore

4) Gut and Psychology Syndrome, Dr. Natasha Campbell, McBride

CHAPTER 5

1) A Smart Women's Guide to Weight Loss, Lorna, R. Vanderhaeghe, M.S., Headlines Promotions Ltd.

2) Time Magazine, Sept. 12, 2011

3) Stop Prediabetes Now, Jack Challem, John Wiley and Sons, 2007

4) Nutrition Reporter, Sept. 2008, Vol. 19, #9

5) The Carbohydrate Addict's Diet, Drs. Rachel and Richard Heller, Signet Book, 1993

6) The Nutrition Reporter, July 2011, Vol.22, #7

7) The Nutrition Reporter, November 2009, Vol. 20, #11

8) Nutrition Reporter, April 2010, Vol. 21, #4

CHAPTER 6

1) Natural News.com, June 16/2011

2) The Nutrition Reporter, January 2009, Vol.20, #1

3) Eggs, Dietary Friend or Foe, Louise Chang, MD. Web MD.

4) The Nutrition Reporter, March, 2006, Vol. 17, #3

5) The Gold Coast Cure, Andrew Larson, MD, (HCL, 2006)

6) Natural News.com, Sept 7/2011

7) Time Magazine, Sept. 12/2011

CHAPTER 9

1) Ultra Wellness.com, 2010

2) The Nutrition Reporter, July 2002, Vol. 13, #7

3) Nutra Ingredients.com, May 2008

4) www.pycnogenol.com, Research news, March 2004

5) Breaking News on Supplements and Nutrition, June 2011

6) Nutra Ingredients.com, Sept. 2007

7) Nutra Ingredients.com March 2008

8) The Nutrition Reporter, March 2008, Vol. 19, #3

9) The Nutrition Reporter, Feb. 2007, Vol. 18, #2

Index

A

B

C

D

E

F

V

W

DoGood
Consulting